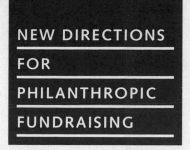

NEW DIRECTIONS
FOR
PHILANTHROPIC
FUNDRAISING

W9-APR-114

Timothy L. Seiler
The Center on Philanthropy at Indiana University

Cathlene Williams
Association of Fundraising Professionals

EDITORS

DIVERSITY IN THE FUNDRAISING PROFESSION

Janice Gow Pettey
Sacramento Regional Foundation

EDITOR

NUMBER 34, WINTER 2001

DIVERSITY IN THE FUNDRAISING PROFESSION
Janice Gow Pettey (ed.)
New Directions for Philanthropic Fundraising, No. 34, Winter 2001
Timothy L. Seiler, Cathlene Williams, Editors

NEW DIRECTIONS FOR PHILANTHROPIC FUNDRAISING is indexed in Higher Education
Abstracts and Philanthropic Index.

Microfilm copies of issues and articles are available in 16 mm and 35 mm, as well as
microfiche in 105 mm, through University Microfilms Inc., 300 North Zeeb Road,
Ann Arbor, Michigan 48106-1346.

ISSN 1072-172X   ISBN 0-7879-5833-6

NEW DIRECTIONS FOR PHILANTHROPIC FUNDRAISING is part of the Jossey-Bass
Nonprofit and Public Management Series and is published quarterly by Wiley Sub-
scription Services, Inc., A Wiley Company, at Jossey-Bass, 989 Market Street, San
Francisco, California 94103-1741.

SUBSCRIPTIONS cost $75.00 for individuals and $147.00 for institutions, agencies, and
libraries. Prices subject to change. Refer to the order form at the back of this issue.

EDITORIAL CORRESPONDENCE should be sent to Timothy L. Seiler, The Center on
Philanthropy, Indiana University, 550 West North Street, Suite 301, Indianapolis,
IN 46202-3162, or to Cathlene Williams, Association of Fundraising Professionals,
1101 King Street, Suite 700, Alexandria, VA 22314.

www.josseybass.com

Printed in the United States of America on acid-free recycled paper containing at
least 20 percent postconsumer waste.

Contents

Editor's Notes

PRIOR ISSUES of *New Directions for Philanthropic Fundraising* have explored the culture of giving among diverse groups. Diversity in the fundraising profession opens a dialogue on the opportunities and obligations for fundraising practitioners to incorporate culture and tradition into the practice of fundraising. The authors of the five chapters in this volume reflect on either distinctions of diversity from within the profession or observations on strategies to enhance diversity in the nonprofit sector.

In Chapter One S. Sanae Tokumura examines prospect research, cultivation, and solicitation practices, using Hawaii, the first "majority minority" state in the union, as the backdrop. She contrasts the illustrations of ethnic fundraising in Hawaii with excerpts from interviews with colleagues in the continental United States and Canada.

Chapter Two, by Kay C. Peck, is a background essay on the evolution of current gay and lesbian issues combined with examples of appropriate methods for cultivating gay and lesbian donors. Peck cites examples of issues faced by gays and lesbians that illustrate the cultural sensitizing that needs to occur in order to develop successful donor relationships. (Readers looking for quantifiable data on gay and lesbian giving can go to http://www.lgbtfunders.org, the Web site of Funders for Lesbian and Gay Issues, formerly the Working Group on Gay and Lesbian Issues.)

In Chapter Three William F. Bartolini suggests the use of communications strategies in furthering the management of diversity in the workplace. Recognizing diversity as an element of identity and understanding the schemata people use as a form of fostering understanding are central components of this chapter. Recommendations on managing diversity by developing an organizational culture sensitive to and appreciative of diversity are also addressed.

NEW DIRECTIONS FOR PHILANTHROPIC FUNDRAISING, NO. 34, WINTER 2001 © WILEY PERIODICALS, INC.

Maria Gitin examines the importance of diversity in philanthropic boards in Chapter Four. This chapter offers a comprehensive examination of need, motivation, and strategies for diversifying boards. Challenges and limitations are addressed, along with thought-provoking comments on assumptions that limit positive action.

Chapter Five, by Samuel N. Gough, Jr., shifts the focus from the individual to the organization and provides succinct suggestions supporting the need to build inclusiveness into the mission and work of the nonprofit organization. Gough points to differences among women, people of color, and faith-based groups as conditions of diversity.

All of the chapters refer directly or indirectly to the dearth of quantifiable data on diversity, as measured by gifts, categorized by type of donor, or measured by benchmarks for success. The challenge continues for increased research on the subject so that the accumulation of knowledge on successful fundraising in diverse populations is driven by analysis, research, and hard data. With these benchmarks or measures in place, our ability to increase the level of success in diverse philanthropy will grow. We are on the right road. What we need next are signs to direct the way.

Janice Gow Pettey
Editor

JANICE GOW PETTEY *is the author of* Cultivating Diversity in Fundraising *(Wiley, 2001). She is CEO of the Sacramento Regional Foundation and is an adjunct professor at the University of San Francisco, where she teaches fundraising and philanthropy classes. She is a former chief advancement officer for the American Red Cross in the Bay Area and former vice president of development for the YMCA of San Francisco and the United Way of the Bay Area. She is a member of the Association of Fundraising Professionals (AFP), the AFP Ethics Committee, and the AFP Research Council, and is a past chair of the AFP Diversity Committee.*

Ethnicity and cultural tradition must be addressed in the development of successful strategies for fundraising in diverse communities. The ways custom and tradition work to enhance philanthropy are illustrated with examples from Hawaii, the first "majority minority" state.

1

Fundraising mores in diverse communities: The role of ethnicity and culture

S. Sanae Tokumura

IF HUMANITY the world over were the same, fundraisers the world over would have an easy time. If we knew that no variation existed, we would simply apply classic fundraising programs throughout the year, evaluate them responsibly, and do the same thing next year, except maybe more creatively. Perhaps some organizations actually do this, believing that the human beings supporting them are all the same. Most likely, with this approach, their supporters will remain the same forevermore.

The truth is that we live in a world of acknowledged human variety. Centuries of international commerce and other forms of mutual dependence have peopled our own country and communities with generations of families and individuals from all over the world. Anthropologists Alfred Kroeber and Ralph Linton had exposed the myth of cultural homogeneity, of huddled communities of sameness,

NEW DIRECTIONS FOR PHILANTHROPIC FUNDRAISING, NO. 34, WINTER 2001 © WILEY PERIODICALS, INC.

decades ago (Wolf, 1982). Societies have continued to intersect, develop, and proliferate because of interactions between each other throughout history. In the mingling, societies have become stronger.

In America the idea of societal sameness and conventionality is fast becoming "last season" and is giving way to the media-enforced vogue of individuality, diversity, and uniqueness. America's societal constant is rapid change, and our systems rev to keep up with dizzying corresponding adaptations in product development, marketing, business practice, lawmaking, education, adopted traditions, blended language, and accepted and politically correct worldviews. Anthropologists tell us that such "mingling is not recent, but dates right back to the period of the great European explorers and long before" (Carrithers, 1997, p. 100). As this scientific observation ripples past the conventions of our civilization, its reality finally begins to fall upon us, and we begin to surf its applications in our area.

In the world of philanthropy in America, excitement is building as fundraisers discover "donors of color" or "minority philanthropy" (Anft, 2001). In its 2000–01 drive the Los Angeles United Way targeted major gifts from non-Euro-American philanthropists as a focus among other less pursued sources of support and became one of the few United Ways that experienced an increase in contributions from the prior year. Asian American Dominic Ng, president of East West Bancorp, solicited many of those major gifts (Fix, 2001).

Advancing Philanthropy ("International Fundraising," 2001) reported growing professional interest in international fundraising. Globalization of the fundraising profession further emphasizes our need to understand the complexity of diverse communities, attitudes toward giving, and the unique history of individuals who will be asked to contribute resources toward their own communities' needs and to those of others. The opportunity to advance our understanding of this concept presents itself not only overseas but also right here in our American backyard.

During my fundraising career in Hawaii, America's fiftieth state, I was involved in repairing several campaigns that were harmed by well-meaning but culturally challenged fundraisers who hailed from several of our forty-nine other states. As I resuscitated key funding relationships and conducted damage control public relations programming, I had the dubious privilege of hearing firsthand from philanthropists who told consistent stories of being "turned off" by "that *haole* fundraiser" and that "typical East Coast style." *Haole* is a Hawaiian word popularly used in Hawaii's general population to refer to any person of European descent. Depending on how it is spoken and in what context, it could be simply a harmless descriptive word or an offensive racial slur. Pukui and Elbert (1986, p. 58) define the term this way: "[t]o act like a white person, to ape the white people, or assume airs of superiority."

Relationships that had been carefully cultivated for years by respected organizations had been swept away by careless actions or words by fundraisers who were misinterpreted as being deliberately rude or offensive. Each situation involved cultural misunderstanding or a sense of ethnic offense and was never mission or case related. Each resulted in at least the disinterest, or at worst total alienation, of a donor, volunteer, or staff member. Each situation involved an enthusiastic, competent, sophisticated Euro-American fundraiser, a fiscally responsible organization, solid case statement, and an annual donor constituency of diverse ethnic and cultural background, mostly Asian. What went wrong? Given indisputable case statements and impressive annual reports, what is the key to cultivating and soliciting a major prospective Asian American philanthropist? In the larger picture, what is the significance of ethnicity and culture in the fundraising relationship? What do ethnicity and culture have to do with matters between a solicitor and a philanthropist?

Although there are different approaches to the definition of *ethnicity*, throughout this chapter I am using a general definition by Walter P. Zenner (1996). He defines ethnicity as seeing oneself and being seen by others as part of a group on the basis of presumed ancestry. Common features that ethnic groups share may be racial, religious, linguistic, occupational, or regional. Important to the discussion, however, are Sokolovskii and Tishkov's descriptions (1997) of the three approaches to defining ethnicity. These authors explain the primordialist, instrumentalist, and constructivist approaches: primordialist theories state that ethnic identification is based on primordial attachments to a group; instrumentalists treat ethnicity as a political instrument exploited by leaders in pursuit of their own interests; and constructivists believe that total ethnic identity is fluid and made in specific social and historical contexts. This third view is consistent with what I believe is occurring in American society today.

Regarding the term *culture* in this chapter, I refer to the perspective defined by anthropologists as "the complex whole which includes knowledge, belief, art, morals, law, custom and any other capabilities and habits acquired by man as a member of society" (Carrithers, 1997, p. 98).

Within the larger frame of global societal development, we are just beginning to notice shifts in the critical field of philanthropy. Fundraising professionals need to adjust worldviews, attitudes, and practices accordingly. This chapter will explore the role ethnicity and culture play in the personal, major gift philanthropic relationship, using Hawaii as an informal laboratory. A collection of impressions from individuals representative of the largest non-Euro-American ethnic groups in Hawaii regarding solicitation experiences will be shared. Seasoned colleagues from the United States and Canada will also offer their observations of the role ethnic and cultural understanding plays in the fund development relationship in their range of experiences.

In conclusion, I will suggest that there are established, unwritten fundraising mores in most communities throughout our country. These mores are ever present but shifting, because the individuals that people these communities bring into the philanthropic equation not only their learned ethnic behaviors but also the evolving history and resulting internal ethnicity of the region itself (Carrithers, 1997; Zenner, 1996). Regarding the real approach of philanthropists from these diverse ethnic and cultural backgrounds, I will offer one of our basic rules. In addition, I will emphasize a new facet of that rule that has developed in our changing field. The basic rule is this: thorough major gift prospect research conducted prior to contact is essential to building a productive relationship with any major prospective donor. The emphasis is the following: acknowledgment of and respect for the ethnic and cultural background of a prospective donor leads toward a desired environment of trust that is required for the consideration of a major gift, a fact requiring that donor research must also now include the "cultural collateral" of the prospective philanthropist. Such preparation will most likely significantly increase the success percentage in cultivation and solicitation of philanthropists of ethnically and culturally diverse backgrounds. *Cultural collateral* is a term I use to refer to an individual's ethnicity, age, gender, educational level, and social position. In practice, the advantage of working with local volunteers and staff directly familiar and comfortable with the cultural collateral of major gift prospects of diverse backgrounds is incalculable.

A foundation for beliefs and practice

A product of three generations of acculturation and assimilation in Hawaii's unique social environment, I identify myself first as a Christian American mother with Buddhist values, second as a fundraiser, and, oh yes—a wife. I hardly think of my ancestral background unless filling out a form that asks for my ethnic grouping. In my youth I grew up blind to most ethnic differences.

I had to learn from schoolbooks and oral history that about a hundred years ago my people departed the Land of the Rising Sun for the territory of Hawaii, what they called *Tenjiku*, or Lord Buddha's paradise. Like most immigrants of the day, they were young, brave, hopeful risk takers, bold in their independence, exhilarated by the opportunities *Tenjiku* and the sugar plantations promised. Along with immigrant dreams, Japanese brought to Hawaii values of *on* and *giri*, or gratitude and obligation, besides traditions, music, sushi, and karate. They taught my American-born parents that education was of primary importance, that honesty, loyalty, courtesy, and industry would earn them respect and their families honor. Sacrificing personal comforts, they eked out a future for my parents on wages of a dollar a day. They educated them and sent sons to fight against Japan and the Nazis in World War II, sons never to be seen again. Those young men and their compatriots eventually earned for all Americans of Japanese ancestry the statement from President Harry S. Truman "You have fought not only the enemy, but you have fought prejudice—and you have won." Truman uttered this inspiration in 1945 in an address at a White House ceremony that honored the 100th Battalion and 442nd Regimental Combat Team. These units were the most decorated of their size in U.S. Army history. Chang's *I Can Never Forget* (1991) broke ground in finally reflecting taciturn Japanese American soldiers' personal views and experiences of World War II.

Out of a state population of approximately 1,156,014, Japanese Americans now are Hawaii's second largest non-European ethnic group, with about 211,364 residents. That population is exceeded by the Hawaiian and part-Hawaiian group at 254,910 and is followed by about 141,696 Filipinos, 47,103 Chinese, and 11,510 Koreans. Caucasians number approximately 237,019 (Department of Business, 2000). Asian Americans today hold positions of political and economic power in the fiftieth state. Many, many of these individuals are capable of making or influencing significant, lasting tributes and six-figure and greater cash gifts to charities that solicit their philanthropy properly.

In my approach to philanthropists of these backgrounds today, there are obvious benefits to sharing similar family histories. I have observed that the trust level of major philanthropic investors that is a prerequisite to the granting of any gift increases dramatically to a state of heroic philanthropic commitment when at least one of the solicitors of a team can strike a chord of ethnic commonality or acknowledgment of cultural understanding between parties. This chord is heard in the individual's core, heart, or soul—the place where such subjects as devotion, obligation, sacrifice, honor, gratitude, and philanthropy are contemplated. For many Asian Americans in Hawaii, their worldviews begin with knowledge of the sacrifices of those who came before them.

Immigrant seeding in the islands began with the need for large numbers of low-skilled workers for Hawaii's developing sugar industry in the 1850s. By the 1860s sugar had become the backbone of the Hawaiian economy (Kuykendall, 1953). In full control of government by the end of the nineteenth century, plantation owners demanded compliant labor forces. This demand became a matter of foreign policy with the creation of the Bureau of Immigration, which became responsible for the massive immigration of Polynesian, Japanese, German, Portuguese, and Norwegian laborers to Hawaii between 1864 and 1893.

The very first major Asian immigrants to *Tan Heung Shan*, or "Sandalwood Mountains" as the Chinese called Hawaii, were South Chinese (Glick, 1980). They began arriving in force in 1852. Most of the migrants filled labor requirements for sugar plantations, and others began enterprises as merchants and craftsmen. Chinese rapidly dispersed throughout Honolulu to form various societies and ties with native Hawaiians and the rest of the Hawaiian community. By the time the monarchy was overthrown in 1893, children of these immigrants born in Hawaii moved on to higher economic, social, and political levels. Although Euro-Americans controlled the sugar plantations, government, and larger businesses, Hawaii-educated children of established Chinese immigrants snatched up opportunities in the independent trades and small businesses created by booming economic expansion in the islands. Gradually, as Chinese assimilated into Hawaiian society, traditions and cultural values of the Chinese assimilated into the general community as well. According to Glick, by 1898 an estimated forty-six thousand Chinese had migrated to the islands.

Chinese became active as early as the mid-1800s in the general Hawaiian community by participating as a distinctive ethnic group in community-wide activities. Close relations with the native

Hawaiian group characterized their earlier assimilation period. Chinese-Hawaiian marriages were common. Although the first priority for Chinese philanthropy had always been their "own sick, needy, and aged," through their organized societies, their status in Hawaii's mainstream quickly grew with their participation in many philanthropic activities for concerns that went beyond their own. It was this philanthropy that earned the Chinese entry into the mainstream social network of old Hawaii (Glick, 1980). Chinese culture became a source of Chinese American pride when Hawaii began to showcase its ethnic diversity.

Original Japanese missed their homeland's cultural traditions and soon were able to create venues to enjoy their music, dance, foods, language, and religion. Because of their large numbers, they were able to maintain homeland customs and insulate themselves against "new country" change forces. Second-generation World War II Japanese vigorously attempted to deny their ethnicity, and many even changed their Japanese first names to American names. After the war many of these second-generation Japanese reaffirmed their ethnic background, feeling a kind of cultural remorse and some resentment at being treated poorly by their country despite their patriotism and supreme sacrifices during the war.

Powerful Euro-American plantation forces continued their attempts to secure tractable, hardworking migrant workers who would be content to live and work on the plantations. After the Japanese wave that landed 140,457 immigrants on Hawaii's shores between 1852 and 1909 (Hawaiian Sugar Technologists, 1950), Korean immigrants were the next largest Asian group to arrive, beginning in 1903 (Patterson, 2000).

Plantation owners were concerned that Japanese laborers constituted nearly two-thirds of the planters' workforce. Because the Japanese were prone to organizing illegal strikes and work stoppages, planters focused on the problem of maintaining a racial mix to prevent one race from dominating labor. Unable to depend on Chinese labor as a result of the 1882 Chinese Exclusion Act, plantation owners looked to the Koreans to offset Japanese numbers. By 1905 about 5,000 of about 7,500 Korean immigrants were working on sugar plantations in Hawaii and constituted 11 percent of the labor force, compared with the Japanese at 66 percent and the Chinese at 9 percent (U.S. Department of Commerce and Labor, 1911). Immigrants from the Korean group were from mixed social positions. Unlike the Japanese and most of the Chinese, who were farmers, a small but significant number of these Korean immigrants were educated and from the upper class (Patterson, 2000).

Because of their smaller numbers, Koreans needed to associate with others of different ethnic and cultural backgrounds and became acculturated to the Western lifestyle more quickly. According to Patterson (2000, p. 33), "Second generation Koreans recorded one of the highest rates of professionalization; both first and second generation Koreans exhibited more liberal and egalitarian attitudes toward social issues than Chinese or Japanese; by the time second generation Koreans reached maturity in the 1960s and 1970s, they had achieved the highest per capita income and the lowest unemployment rate of any ethnic group in Hawaii, including Caucasians."

Fifteen Filipinos arrived in the Territory in December 1906 in order to stake out Hawaii sugar plantation living conditions and report back to prospective migrants. By 1920 a steady stream of Filipino workers began arriving in Hawaii. Numbers of migrants peaked between 1922 and 1929 (Anderson, Coller, and Pestano, 1984). Plantation owners were happiest with this uncomplaining, hardworking, stable group.

Filipinos, who in their native land were separated by demarcations of family, district, and region, began to draw together in Hawaii for strength and safety (Anderson, Coller, and Pestano, 1984). A great need for a feeling of security was felt on arrival, as the immigrants received "condescending and even somewhat repressive treatment" from Hawaii's general community (Anderson, Coller, and Pestano, 1984, p. 109). A common understanding among the Filipino family and friend groups is about mutual obligation. It is this bind that still holds the Filipino community together in alliances of workers, neighbors, relatives, or friends. A strong sense of belonging and recognition of "outsiders" pervades these alliances. Early Filipinos tended to be willing to discard their cultural identity when confronted with a choice to do so. Not so with the later Filipino generation, born after 1946, which shared a sense of fierce pride in their language, traditions, and people. Recent immigrants are socially distinct from Hawaiian-born Filipinos and prefer traditional cultural practices, whereas Hawaiian-born counterparts prefer to be involved with Hawaii's unique Americanized culture. The most recent immigrants, highly educated with a good command of the English language, are fast emerging as leaders in their attempts to retain cultural identity.

The four major Asian immigrant groups experienced some similarities in adjustment and acculturation in their new home. Each original group shared a diligent work ethic and today fiercely values educational opportunities for their children. Each original group valued humility and frowned on those in their number who desired advancement and status too keenly (Anderson, Coller, and Pestano, 1984). Korean immigrants and Hawaiian-born Chinese, Japanese, and Koreans feel this need to justify success to their cultural groups less than the Filipinos. Group identity after the second generation is much less important to Asian Americans. Filial loyalty, however, remains a priority for most individuals among the Asians in Hawaii.

Breathing

For non-Euro-American fundraisers or fundraisers immersed in diverse ethnic and cultural environments such as Hawaii, describing and analyzing the phenomenon of relationship building with philanthropists of these ethnic backgrounds is like studying our breathing at different altitudes. Recognition of diversity is not contemplated or studied by the diverse but lived, felt, and honored instantaneously. Working in this environment involves adjustment, and that adjustment is unconscious and natural.

My normal visits with various philanthropists and communities on different islands in Hawaii involve adapting like a chameleon to different presentation and conversation styles, social graces, and even appropriate attire several times a day. Whole-day seminars could be created around how to approach one group or another, and yet these truths are philanthropic mores to those of us who easily and successfully practice in Hawaii's unique cultural environment.

On the other hand, in discussions with philanthropists of color and leading fundraisers alike, this adjusting interaction that is innate to some may be puzzling, intriguing, mysterious, specialized, or worse, troublesome, altogether avoided, or of no concern, to most otherwise sophisticated fundraisers. Some fundraisers deny that there should be any difference in how all Americans should be treated in the solicitation process. If fundraisers seem removed from awareness of ethnic or cultural "sensitivities" in the philanthropic setting, either they may be educated to understand the ideal that humanity is all the same and approach all people in that open way, or they may be simply physically removed from diverse communities and not exposed to the people who lived through periods of time in which they were actively discriminated against.

Originally, cultural science intended to support tolerance and mutual understanding between societies (Carrithers, 1997). Perhaps as we become more educated in this way, we live the ideals we have learned, and that is good. Yet there still remain several generations that remember differently, and it is also good to know this. In addition, there are those who were never educated and continue to discriminate against individuals of diverse backgrounds, and this behavior perpetuates the negative perceptions held by those discriminated against.

In my work I use the standards and ethics of our profession equally, exercising research, programming, implementation, and evaluation precisely from one organization to the next, with all their varied constituencies. However, in the design of *approach* in major gift programs and campaigns, each individual philanthropic prospect is carefully evaluated and matched, with attention to ethnicity and cultural background, with appropriate volunteers and staff for cultivation purposes. Behavior and communication styles adjust with organization staff and boards as well.

Historical documents during the early immigration years refer to open demarcations between ethnic groups. Franck (1937, p. 12), writing on the Filipino and Japanese immigrant, demonstrates typical views of the time: "They are confirmed knife-toters and much given to fighting over women, who are scarce among them. It is a common saying in Hawaii that 'the Filipino is only one pair of pants removed from the jungle.' And that pair is likely to be purple or strawberry-red or wine-colored or something of that sort, topped by shirts—on gala days whole suits—that make a rainbow seem colorless. 'Japanese steal big: Filipinos steal little,' is another island saying."

In 1989 young Japanese American lawyer Bruce Yamashita was pressured out of the U.S. Marine Corps officer candidate school. "You speak English?" "We don't want your kind," and "[In World War II] we whipped your Japanese ass" were statements he reported hearing (Chang, 1991, p. 199).

With this recent a history of such perceptions and receptions, approaching a prospect of Filipino or Japanese ancestry in Hawaii with an unprepared Euro-American volunteer, staff member, or consultant using conventional solicitation methods is ill advised.

How is it that some fundraisers are able to adjust to diverse philanthropic markets easily and naturally and others are gripped with uncertainty, fear, and loathing at the prospect of cultivating or soliciting prospective philanthropists of diverse ethnic and cultural backgrounds? For those of us who were fortunate enough, we went to Hawaii's "diversity school" or sister schools throughout the country.

Hawaii's diversity school

Diversity school began for us in the islands well before we hit the alphabet. In the 1960s on the island of Kauai, the northernmost and oldest of the Hawaiian Islands, grass sliding on cardboard box panels behind Lihue baseball field was the hottest thing for those less than a certain age, and the age boundary was not absolute. My co-sliders were other Americans of Filipino, Portuguese, Chinese, *haole*, Hawaiian, and *hapa* (mixtures of any of those) backgrounds. Many of us never knew what we were, and none of us knew the meaning of Truman's or anyone else's prejudice. As long as you shared the cardboard, you were OK.

The story of my uncle Tsutomu's supreme sacrifice in World War II (I had never met him), when the dinosaurs still roamed the earth, was accepted as easily as my newest bike or hula hoop and with an innocent attitude of entitlement. From youth my "chop suey" friends (local Hawaiian slang meaning "many different and mixed") shared folktales, food, music, and customs and learned the distinctive pidginized language of Kauai, which today can even be heard in boardrooms there at unguarded moments.

Quietly, naturally, my friends and I learned the unique conglomerate traditions and attitudes that were the cultural fabric of our unique Garden Island society. Interestingly, those outside that knowledge were given "outsider" status.

I still do not have difficulty telling the difference visibly between a "local" Korean, Japanese, or Chinese person, nor do I care. My third generation of purged perceptions, however, is vastly different from the extremely prejudiced views of first-generation immigrants, who carried their fear and resentment of each other with them to our island paradise.

And as years passed, I experienced firsthand the subtle (and sometimes not so subtle) discrimination and prejudice in Hawaii that exist in our renowned atmosphere of ethnic diversity. Although my eager childhood color blindness left me along with my childhood, memories and, somehow, the unquestioned acceptance of various peoples, with all their differences, remain. We may be one more generation closer to just sharing the cardboard but are not there yet, even in Hawaii.

Birth of a fundraiser

With my hand on my heart, I can say the following is true: when most of my preschool counterparts were being asked to spell *cat* by their moms or dads as we began to learn our language skills, my mother Fusae was asking me to spell *eleemosynary*. She always asked me to define it, too. Today my professional life revolves around the meaning of my first spelling word.

The first decade of my fundraising career was spent on the staffs of three major nonprofits in Hawaii. The first two, with their strong constituencies of Japanese American supporters, benefited very quickly from philanthropic relationships I had the pleasure of helping to begin, cultivate, and bring to fruition. To this day those generous individuals and businesses continue to support those charities. The second decade, now just ended, was exciting and richly meaningful, spent in independent consultation with a variety of organizations. Constituencies may differ, but strategy adjustments in volunteer training, board development, campaign planning, and major donor cultivation and solicitation are easy, natural, and successful. Going to one of the best diversity schools in the world was perfect background for my chosen profession. One of the most essential discoveries I made was that each prospective contributor has unique cultural collateral.

Cultural collateral

The unique ethnicity and ethnic history of a prospective philanthropist, along with the prospect's age, gender, and social position, constitute the notes of a unique chord I call "cultural collateral." Awareness and understanding of, and sensitivity to, this blend of unwritten, unspoken information are critical in the process of cultivating and soliciting a major philanthropic prospect of any ethnic background. When planning the approach to philanthropists of diverse ethnic backgrounds in Hawaii, it is absolutely mandatory to consider not only the gift potential and philanthropic proclivity of the prospect but also the prospect's cultural collateral. The prospect's cultural collateral is similar to the collateral we all present about our causes and organizations at our critical meetings, except that the prospect's cultural collateral is not printed, taped, or communicated in any fixed way. This unique information is resonated heart to heart, and woe to the fundraiser who is deaf to its messages. The true sounding of this chord rapidly creates an environment of trust in a philanthropic relationship, the trust between organization and prospective philanthropist that is a prerequisite to the development of a major gift. Graduates of diversity schools develop the ability to sense and sound this chord naturally in interactions with a variety of people of diverse backgrounds.

Ethnicity and ethnic history

A relatively new term, *ethnicity* was coined after the 1950s. Zenner's definition (1996) that seeing oneself and being seen by others as part of a group on the basis of presumed ancestry describes a basic sense of ethnicity. Common features that ethnic groups share may be racial, religious, linguistic, occupational, or regional.

In Hawaii and other diverse communities, individuals from various ethnic groups may have issued from different ancestors but share similar religions and occupations, live in similar regions, and share a common pidgin language. In a sense, Hawaii has developed an "internal ethnicity," a condition described by Zenner (1996) as being wholly distinct from anywhere else in the world. In addition, the power of understanding each ethnic group in the context of respective histories in the islands cannot be understated. Names of ancestors, links to families, and the ability to "talk story" (a Hawaiian colloquialism that means to converse in a relaxed fashion) are part of the ritual of relationship cultivation in Hawaii. Knowing history is useful in talking story.

Hawaii's separate islands highlight regional differences that may make it even more difficult for a fundraiser unfamiliar with the state and its people to navigate a relationship. For example, the island of Kauai is for the most part rural and deceptively simple. However, its east-side-based power structure is highly intelligent, politically astute, and fiercely protective of the island's natural resources and humble people. A quiet power on the north shore, wealthy Euro-Americans have transplanted themselves, attracted to Kauai's spiritual and physical beauty. Altogether, Kauai's people tend to suspect "outsiders" and are quick to recognize avarice and insincerity.

Maui, more urbanized, can be likened to a mainland city such as San Diego. Its people are intensely proud of its relative economic success as compared with the rest of the state. Residents respect the independent and superior planning of Maui's leaders and believe the rest of the state would benefit if it followed Maui's lead. Although the rest of the state marvels at Maui's success, neighbor islands also fear the possibility of their communities evolving into "mainlandlike" Maui and strive to conserve old Hawaii's character.

The Big Island of Hawaii can be separated into three major regions that all sport different "personalities." Hilo, on the eastern shore, is the center of commerce on the island, where the island's seat of government is located and many of the island's oldest families reside. Hilo residents may be a bit friendlier and more open than Kauai people, but they are very similar. Kona, directly west of Hilo, is a resort area composed of Kailua residents, who are largely transplanted Euro-Americans, and the *mauka* (a Hawaiian word meaning "mountain") residents, who are older, established descendants of original Japanese immigrants. Waimea, to the north, is an intimate, health-centered, wealthy ranching community.

The beautiful and remote islands of Lanai and Molokai are largely left alone, as their residents are few. However, rural and scenic, the neighbor isles of Hawaii have recently been attracting the rich and famous from all walks of life and generations as part-time residents. As these prospective philanthropists become more involved in their communities, they will add yet another interesting dimension to Hawaii's complex internal ethnicity. Currently, the newest "snowbirds" choose to hibernate privately and for the most part prefer to apply their philanthropy to their hometown needs.

Oahu is Hawaii's center of commerce and government. Neighbor island residents consider Honolulu a big city. Urban Oahu residents are frequently accused by neighbor islanders of not respecting the systems and professionals on the neighbor isles, being generally condescending, and disregarding the needs and distance disadvantages of neighbor isle businesses and branches.

Age

Elders, or those in Hawaii who are wise and learned, are called *kupuna* in Hawaiian. When moving in Hawaii's philanthropic circles, *kupuna* volunteers of higher social stature can obtain audiences with prospective philanthropists more easily because it is a social obligation to show respect and deference to *kupuna*. All Asian groups in Hawaii will recognize the value of harnessing the wisdom of their elders in planning for a stronger community. Frequently, commemorative giving opportunities for parents or grandparents will appeal to an Asian donor who eschews personal recognition for reasons explained in this chapter. Sacrifices of the original immigrants will be revered and respected by the adults of each ethnic group in Hawaii.

Gender

When I was a young vice president for development on the staff of a nonprofit, my male (Asian) secretary and I arrived at a meeting at the Hawaii office of a Japanese corporation. He was immediately and happily seated in a more respected position at the conference table. When our identities were determined, our hosts were mortified and switched our seats immediately. Knowledge of the role of gender in various ethnic groups can be useful in the cultivation of philanthropists of diverse background. Asian groups may give the impression that their women are deferential to men. However, more often than not, it is the woman who will influence philanthropic decisions and who should definitely not be left out of such discussions.

Social position

Anderson, Coller, and Pestano (1984) describe status considerations as going far beyond education or personal wealth for Filipinos. Similarly for the other Asian groups, family history and honorable conduct, leadership in community concerns, and other subtle areas create status. It is therefore important to identify such opinion leaders as well as the wealthy in feasibility studies for major campaign planning in order to engage the group properly. Knowledge of a prospective philanthropist's social position is necessary in order to assign the most appropriate volunteer to begin cultivation and to solicit major gifts. Asian languages reflect the critical nature of social position by assigning several levels of honorific pronouns and idioms that denote propriety of address regarding age, gender, and social rank. This sense of propriety has not altered much in Asian groups despite generations of Westernization in Hawaii.

The science of trust

During a cultivation visit or solicitation appointment, information rapidly passes between solicitor and prospect. While the case for support is being made and organizational collateral is being presented, the prospect is also presenting information. Part of the prospect's information is unspoken, unwritten cultural collateral. The solicitor receives this information, processes it, and responds. The first few minutes of this multilevel exchange greatly determine for the prospect whether the solicitor is worthy of attention and trust.

According to Gibb (1978, pp. 14–23) trust works powerfully among members of ethnic groups and functions as a "lubricant of individual and social life." He goes on to describe trust as a dismantler of the defensive instinct that looks for motives or hidden meanings. On the other hand, lack of trust causes us to look for strategies in dealing with each other, seek help from others, and look for protection in rules and the law; ebbing of trust results in alienation and hostility. Unstrategized and freely given trust promotes motivation, energy, perception, emotion, cognition, action, and synergy according to Friedlander (1970). A state of trust occurs most readily between individuals who view each other as having similar values. If, as Herskovits (1972) views it, values are greatly based on ethnic and cultural learning, those of us interested in establishing trust must learn about the individual or group with which we hope to establish relationships in this way.

International business strategies

In Hawaii each ethnic group has contributed not only to developing its distinct culture in the islands but also to developing a conglomerate internal ethnicity that distinguishes Hawaiian society.

For a greater understanding of how to approach this complexity, fundraisers can look to social and anthropological sciences for background as well as to the private sector. For years global industries have worked to understand diversity of cultures and ethnic groups in order to press forward in foreign lands. Industries have discovered that each culture has its own ways of developing relationships and negotiating. It is understood that venturing into unfamiliar territories without first understanding clients' or employees' cultural collateral is to fail (Trompenaars, 1994).

A host of guides exist in the international business genre that at the very least describe the great amount of care required to meet a person of Asian background properly and develop a fruitful relationship with such an individual. Engholm's *When Business East Meets Business West* (1991), Hall and Hall's *Hidden Differences* (1987), Leppert's *Doing Business with Korea* (1996), and Parker Pen Company's *Do's and Taboos Around the World* (1993) are good examples of books in which authors cover etiquette, protocol, misconceptions, body language, negotiation, hostess gifts, and other areas.

Hawaii's local suggestions

Chinese are not "huggy-kissy" people, an anonymous Chinese American opinion leader said recently (interview, Nov. 11, 2001). "In Hawaii everybody is huggy-kissy," this opinion leader said. "I'm never sure anymore whether I should shake the hand or be ready to be hugged and kissed by people who come to my office." Although a kiss on the cheek and a hug are accepted in Hawaii as a greeting, this person carries antibacterial lotion so that a quick clean up can be done even after a round of shaking hands. The leader went on to say that wealthy Chinese American associates are difficult to gain audiences with unless introduced by "one of their own." A nearly nonexistent case can win a major gift if presented by a familiar, well-liked colleague.

A third-generation Asian philanthropist married to a Euro-American, Peter Yukimura is president of KOA Trading Company and a recognized business leader on Kauai. Yukimura is concerned with approach styles used on the island by some professional fundraisers. Yukimura related the following experience (interview, Nov. 13, 2001): "This person came to see me; he's dressed like a 'local.' I respected the organization that hired him, so I let him in my office. I don't get bogged down with details and leave that part to others to handle, but I key on the person who is delivering this information, and he definitely turned me off. He didn't know me and presumed I would care about his organization more than all the others I supported. I felt he was condescending. His attitude offended me. He wasn't interested in knowing me, and just gave his canned speech."

Barry Taniguchi is third-generation Japanese American and president and CEO of KTA Super Stores, the Big Island's largest locally owned supermarket chain. He is a CPA and an active leader at his Buddhist temple. Recognized as being one of the most active philanthropists on the island, Taniguchi said that he could sense instantly when a fundraiser is appreciative of his ethnic background and acknowledges the mores of local culture and, on the other hand, when a person is insincere. "It's the attitude," said Taniguchi. "If they take me for granted and expect a 'yes' without knowing my background, the reason our company supports our community, that's a turn-off. My trust level is higher and my commitment is higher when I like the person. This relationship is more important than the numbers shown to me. I can sense a humble, grateful, learning attitude or an arrogant one. Also, having a local person involved in a solicitation team is important, no matter what part of the island the philanthropist is from. It just works better that way" (interview, Nov. 14, 2001).

Edward Choi is third-generation Korean American and president of Edsung Foodservice Co. Son of one of Hawaii's most generous philanthropists, he claims that Koreans in Hawaii are not a well-activated philanthropic resource as yet. "Generally Hawaii Koreans have a lot of money but tend to be more scrutinizing of who we support, and we're very conservative," he said. "Plus, no one really asks properly" (interview, Nov. 15, 2001). Choi indicated that he receives "zillions" of requests via direct mail and telephone. Although his late father Sungdai was a well-known philanthropist in Hawaii for many years, Edward Choi's involvement in charitable organizations has never been cultivated. *He has never been approached personally* for support.

Rose Churma is acting executive director of the Filipino Community Center. Churma, first-generation Filipino American and a professional architect, explained that in Hawaii, Filipinos differ according to generation in how they are motivated and successfully approached. "Those who have just arrived are powerfully motivated by cultural reasons. Professionals who are successful in Hawaii seem to highly consider tax purposes in making contributions," she noted, adding that they are negatively motivated by recognition (interview, Nov. 13, 2001). These professionals give to return favor to the communities who supported their growth of wealth, she said. Locally born Filipinos mostly respond to family-centered solicitation strategies. In all cases, Churma stated, a visitor unfamiliar with the ethnic history and culture of the Filipino in Hawaii has a high probability of inadvertently "turning off" a prospect because of the complexity of the group.

Euro-American independent consultant Marion Penhallow is a fifth-generation "local *haole*" who was born on Maui and grew up on Oahu. With seventeen years of fundraising experience, begun at Cal State Fullerton as associate vice president for development, Marion had to adjust her "mainland style" after returning to work on Kauai. Proving herself on Kauai despite actually being "local" involved demonstrating her respect for the land and its people, and her humility. "My speech patterns naturally change, my body language shifts, when I communicate with North Shore [transplanted] *haoles*, the old timers in Lihue and Kapaa, and the rural Westsiders. All of this of course changes again when speaking to Japanese, Filipino, Chinese, or Korean people, considering their styles and history on the island," Penhallow said (interview, Nov. 14, 2001).

North American consensus

Respect and knowledge of ethnic or cultural identity between parties in a philanthropic relationship lead to creating trust and commitment throughout the donor cultivation process not only in Hawaii but also in areas throughout North America. All professionals consulted indicated that there are fundraising mores involved in the approach that are best understood prior to contact.

Stanley Weinstein, with thirty-two years in the nonprofit sector, is executive vice president of Hartsook & Associates and a second-generation American of Russian Jewish descent. He said, "Above all, successful development professionals must be gifted at forming meaningful relationships. To the extent that the professional understands the complete person—in all of his or her complexities—the prospective supporter will be more likely to bond with both the professional or volunteer and the institution represented. If the prospective supporter perceives visitors as 'strangers' in any sense, success is far less likely" (interview, Nov. 26, 2001).

Weinstein stated bluntly that cultivation of an individual of Jewish background must involve a Jewish fundraiser or volunteer. "And I wouldn't dream of being a fundraiser in New Mexico without knowing rudimentary Spanish," he said (interview, Nov. 26, 2001). Along with learning a bit of the language comes a respect for the culture and knowledge of intrinsic values, he said, such as the importance of honoring family in the Hispanic culture. "Beyond that, establishing a relationship with any person involves basic human communication skills, sensitivity, and a respectful attitude," said Weinstein, acknowledging that some fundraisers, lacking these skills and attitude, will most likely fail, especially in a situation involving diversity and the complexities involved. Weinstein believes that lack of knowledge of culture and ethnicity barriers may be transcended with proper behavior. "The safety net is always being a good listener, having sincere interest in the other person, being sensitive," he said.

Kim Taylor, twelve-year veteran in Canadian fundraising, is senior consultant for DVA Navion, international fundraising consultants based in Calgary. Euro-Canadian Taylor has developed a keen insight into working with native Canadians, including First Nations, Inuit, and Metis, but only through hard-won experience. Early in her career Taylor began establishing relationships across these cultural boundaries for her employer at the time. She remembered innocently visiting a First Nations bandleader-administrator, a level comparable to chief, intending to solicit support for her organization, armed with her "cause and case." "Naively," she said, "I did not understand that racism could occur in the reverse. . . . I was not taken seriously, and the solicitation process was effectively stopped" (interview, Nov. 9, 2001). Taylor applied her experience and adjusted. Recently, she said, "in visiting a wealthy Aboriginal prospect who was reported to be very interested in a program offered by my organization, I invited along a well-respected Aboriginal employee. He included in his packing a gift for the gentleman. We were well received, and my colleague was able to speak eloquently and passionately about the program. . . . Eventually we brought in the leader of the institution . . . to honor the prospect." The pending gift may reach several millions of dollars, reported Taylor.

"Through significant soul searching and personal growth," Taylor explained, "I came to recognize the value of researching more than just the donor's financial means and areas of interest. A successful solicitor must take the time to research the prospect's ethnicity, including religious, linguistic, ancestral, and regional identity, in order to have any chance of success. Some of this research must be done by the solicitor (not the research department) in order to familiarize oneself with the nuances . . . to fully understand the prospect's perspective" (interview, Nov. 9, 2001). Taylor believes that part of knowing the prospect includes knowing who should be part of the team of solicitors: "Unless I already had a relationship . . . I would not approach a person of a particular ethnic group without having as part of my team a member of that ethnic group. I would take the time to know if my team member should be male or female, and if they should be dressed in such a fashion that would signify a linkage in identity to that of the prospect, and if they were rightly placed in that particular society to appeal to the prospect." Taylor said that these considerations should be common sense but indicated that they were not. She also noted that she has witnessed the failure of many solicitations due to what she considered to be a form of ethnocentrism.

In 1997 the Smithsonian Institution hired Franklin S. Odo to create and direct the Asian Pacific American Program. Odo is a third-generation Japanese American, born and raised in Hawaii. In 1997 Odo developed $10,000 in private funding. By 2001, with 2.5 staff members including himself, private support for the Asian Pacific American Program had risen to $1 million. Prior to his arrival the institution had not been involved in raising money for Asian American programs. Odo credits the personal and professional network of contacts he has established throughout his life with helping to ease his way into the fundraising field and allowing him access and reliable introduction to resources (interview, Oct. 29, 2001).

Odo also said that he had the advantage of having developed knowledge of Asian individuals' general cultural collateral throughout his career. A college professor for thirty years prior to moving to Washington, D.C., Odo left his post as chair of the University of Hawaii Ethnic Studies Department to direct his program at the Smithsonian. Most familiar with the Japanese, Chinese, Korean, Filipino, and Native Hawaiian groups, Odo said he had to work hard to gain Southeast Asian and South Asian background knowledge. Odo agreed with Weinstein that in unfamiliar territory, conversation skills are important. "Asking questions to determine commonality, good listening skills, and using your knowledge to respond properly are critical," he said (interview, Oct. 29, 2001). Supporting Taylor's observation, Odo noted that presentation of the case is secondary to sensing and listening when communicating with others of diverse backgrounds.

Lilya Wagner, with seventeen years in fundraising, is associated with the Center on Philanthropy at Indiana University, is a faculty member at the Fund Raising School, which provides fundraising training internationally, and is a frequent speaker and writer on philanthropy, fundraising, and nonprofit management. Wagner supported her colleagues' statements and emphasized, however, that the fundraising professional should be not only sensitive to prospective donors of diverse backgrounds but also knowledgeable of the actual differences that identify the individual ethnically and culturally. "These differences will shape what information the prospect wishes to know and how that information [should be] delivered," said Wagner (interview, Nov. 9, 2001). Now an American citizen, Wagner was born in Estonia. "In some past cases," she said, "my relationship with the prospect and the commonality that we had in both being 'foreign' overcame that lack of knowledge." But, she explained, she lost a donation once when she was unaware of how much time a potential Southeast Asian donor needed to consider a gift and did not understand his preferences for recognition—both culturally based issues. Employing a volunteer or staff person who is intrinsically knowledgeable is a good solution, said Wagner.

Walt Gillette, born in Waverly, New York, is a Euro-American with fifteen years of fundraising experience. He is a major giving consultant with Development Exchange, Inc. Gillette believes that failing to respect the ethnic and regional identity of a prospective donor will inevitably result in behavior that will not fail to offend before any part of the case can be presented. "Meaningfully demonstrating true interest in another's unique ethnicity and beliefs is the cornerstone of the entire relationship-building process," he said (interview, Nov. 14, 2001). The greatest sin of a fundraiser, Gillette said, is not overcoming perceived barriers to communication, turning a blind eye to diversity, perpetuating stereotypical ethnic differences, and, as a result, never beginning the cultivation and not receiving a gift.

Lona M. Farr agrees. A fundraising professional for twenty-nine years, Farr is now principal in Farr Healey Consulting, LLC. An expert in differences between philanthropic practices of people of German heritage and people of Puerto Rican heritage, she reported that Latinos in Pennsylvania (Puerto Ricans and Mexicans in Allentown, Bethlehem, Easton, and Reading) and Pennsylvania Germans do not understand each other. Farr has established that Latinos can be very generous, her research demonstrating that they will most likely support charities that assist their ethnic group. However, Latinos are rarely cultivated by fundraising organizations because fundraisers dismiss them as not philanthropic and continue to ask them for causes in which Latinos have no interest (e-mail to the author, Nov. 7, 2001).

Margaret Guellich is a Euro-American fundraiser with more than twenty-five years of fundraising experience. Director of International Fundraising Partnership at Catholic Relief Services, Guellich specializes in working with countries outside the United States. Guellich brings up the perspective of the solicitor's own ethnic and cultural background in the cultivation-solicitation dynamic. "I need to be very cognizant of the fact that where I come from and what I know and feel about things will affect how I behave toward people. There are adjustments that need to made in that regard as well as keying on the prospect's unique background," she said (interview, Nov. 9, 2001). Also, Guellich noted that the cultural environment of the region in which a prospect resides affects success percentages significantly. For example, there is a marked distinction between northern (wealthy and transient), southern (laid back), and western (very rural) Virginia. Solicitors need to understand these regional differences and alter solicitation styles, Guellich advised.

Similar distinctions exist between areas such as Edmonton (older, quieter, settled) and Calgary (newly wealthy, less formal, youthful) according to Taylor (interview, Nov. 9, 2001). Weinstein discussed Santa Fe (upscale, casual) and Albuquerque (traditional, conservative) (interview, Nov. 26, 2001). Farr described Philadelphia (predominantly English, heavily influenced by Quakers) and Pittsburgh (similar to the Midwest) like two different countries (e-mail to the author, Nov. 7, 2001). Gillette talked about the Bible Belt, where the "'Bubba system' holds sway on all relationships: business, personal, philanthropic." As Gillette explained it, "The system is predicated on the history of familial relationships, which could be expressed as 'My granddaddy did business with his granddaddy [and outsiders aren't welcome]'" (interview, Nov. 14, 2001).

Conclusion

We have become aware of a wave that we perceive is just now approaching, that of "minority philanthropy." In reality, our rather philanthrocentric attitude has blinded us to the fact that societies the world over have enjoyed the benefits of forms of philanthropy for centuries. We are in fact rushing to catch up to our own slow vision, which only now perceives the possibility of a thrilling new ride. Now fundraisers must quickly adjust vision and direction in long-range planning, board development, fundraising programs, volunteer and staff training, solicitation, and issues of ethnic and cultural diversity.

It is possible to involve donors of diverse ethnic and cultural backgrounds in your constituencies of supporters. In order to do so, it is necessary to adjust prospect research, cultivation, and solicitation practices. Thorough understanding of the prospective funder's or funder group's cultural collateral is absolutely required prior to making contact. This highly unique information—racial, religious, linguistic, occupational, and regional—describes the prospect's ethnic background and history. Also, cultural collateral includes the prospect's age, gender, and social position. If possible, recruit local volunteers to advise you on this collateral. Ideally, hire local staff that knows the collateral intrinsically. Also, it is always ideal to bring to cultivation meetings and events a volunteer whose own cultural collateral resembles the prospect's. It is desirable to involve the groups from whom you seek support in your organization at all levels. Significant diversification of funding sources is not possible without inviting the diverse to share a vision and work toward it together.

References

Anderson, R. N., Coller, R., and Pestano, R. F. *Filipinos in Rural Hawaii.* Honolulu: University of Hawaii Press, 1984.

Anft, M. "Raising Money with Sense and Sensibility." *Chronicle of Philanthropy,* Oct. 18, 2001, pp. 21–23.

Carrithers, M. "Culture." In T. Barfield (ed.), *Dictionary of Anthropology.* Oxford, England: Blackwell, 1997.

Chang, T. *I Can Never Forget.* Honolulu: Sigi, 1991.

Department of Business, Economic Development, and Tourism, State of Hawaii. *State of Hawaii Data Book: Statistical Abstract.* Honolulu: State of Hawaii, 2000.

Engholm, C. *When Business East Meets Business West.* New York: Wiley, 1991.

Fix, J. L. "United Way Donations Barely Rise." *Chronicle of Philanthropy,* Aug. 23, 2001, pp. 23–26.

Franck, H. *Roaming in Hawaii*. New York: Stakes, 1937.

Friedlander, F. "The Primacy of Trust as a Facilitator of Further Group Accomplishment." *Journal of Applied Behavioral Science*, 1970, *6*, 387–400.

Gibb, J. R. *Trust: A New View of Personal and Organizational Development*. Los Angeles: Guild of Tutors, 1978.

Glick, C. *Sojourners and Settlers: Chinese Migrants in Hawaii*. Honolulu: University of Hawaii Press, 1980.

Hall, E. T., and Hall, M. R. *Hidden Differences: Doing Business with the Japanese*. New York: Anchor Press, 1987.

Hawaiian Sugar Technologists. *Immigration and Emigration in the Hawaiian Sugar Industry*. Honolulu: Hawaiian Sugar Technologists, 1950.

Herskovits, M. J. *Cultural Relativism: Perspectives in Cultural Pluralism*. New York: Random House, 1972.

"International Fundraising: When Aid Is a World Away." *Advancing Philanthropy: Ideas and Strategies from the Association of Fundraising Professionals*, Sept.-Oct. 2001, pp. 16–19, 40–43.

Kuykendall, R. S. *Hawaiian Kingdom, 1854–1878: Twenty Critical Years*. Honolulu: University of Hawaii, 1953.

Leppert, P. *Doing Business with Korea*. Chula Vista, CA: Jain, 1996.

Parker Pen Company. *Do's and Taboos Around the World*. New York: Wiley, 1993.

Patterson, W. *The Ilse*. Honolulu: University of Hawaii, 2000.

Pukui, M. K., and Elbert, S. H. *Hawaiian Dictionary*. Honolulu: University of Hawaii Press, 1986.

Sokolovskii, S., and Tishkov, V. "Ethnicity." In A. Barnard and J. Spencer (eds.), *Encyclopedia of Social and Cultural Anthropology* (Vol. 1). London: Routledge, 1997.

Trompenaars, F. *Riding the Waves of Culture: Understanding Cultural Diversity in Business*. New York: Irwin, 1994.

U.S. Department of Commerce and Labor, Bureau of Labor. *Fourth Report of the Commissioner of Labor in Hawaii*. Washington, D.C.: U.S. Government Printing Office, 1911.

Wolf, E. *Europe and the People Without History*. Los Angeles: University of California Press, 1982.

Zenner, W. P. "Ethnicity." In D. Levinson and M. Ember (eds.), *Encyclopedia of Cultural Anthropology*. 4 vols. New York: Holton, 1996.

S. SANAE TOKUMURA *is the president of Solid Concepts, Inc., a nonprofit consulting firm based in Honolulu and a member of the board of directors of the Association of Fundraising Professionals.*

Fundraisers and nonprofit organizations will face unique challenges if they begin, for the first time, to address gay individuals and groups as potential donors or populations to be served. Greater understanding of the gay community helps encourage the sensitivity needed to be successful in that effort.

2

Looking at life through rainbow-colored glasses

Kay C. Peck

"IT WAS AWFUL when the police came. It was like a swarm of hornets attacking a bunch of butterflies," said one eyewitness to the beginning of the Stonewall riots on June 27, 1969 (Lisker, 1969, p. 3). Many refer to the Stonewall riots as the birthplace of the modern gay rights movement. They began when police came to make a "routine" raid on a gay bar, but, for whatever reason, the usually passive patrons decided it was time to fight back.

The witness was not one of the patrons of the Stonewall Inn on the evening that triggered days of rioting in the gay, lesbian, bisexual, and transgendered section of Greenwich Village in New York City. That eyewitness was Shirley Evans, a heterosexual mother of two, whose apartment neighbored the Stonewall Inn. She stated that the Stonewall was not a rowdy place and the patrons were never troublesome. "Up until the night of the police raid, there was never any trouble there," she said. "The homosexuals minded their own business and never bothered a soul" (Lisker, 1969, p. 3).

Perhaps this is an apt reminder that homosexuals have never been without friends, even in the most trying of times. What is more, on a scale of one to ten—with the days when gay men were nicknamed "faggot" after the bundles of sticks used to burn them to death being a one and acceptance from friends, family, government, religious institutions, self, and all of society being a ten—today's Western culture is probably as close to a ten as it has ever been for those of nontraditional sexual orientations.

For example, look at the fate of multiple gay-related initiatives in elections throughout the United States in November 2001. Voters in three Michigan cities faced important choices concerning their gay residents. Of the three ballot measures—two to enact discriminatory city charter amendments and one to repeal a civil rights law—all failed by strong margins. Voters in Miami Beach passed a positive effort to support gay residents when Dade County, Florida, voted to extend domestic benefits coverage to same sex partners of employees. In the rash of gay-related issues on 2001 ballots, only one failed to favor gay and lesbian residents. Houston voters approved amending the city charter to prohibit the nation's fourth-largest city from offering domestic partner benefits to municipal employees ("Rights Advocates," 2001). Even the loss in Houston was an indication of positive change. The fact that the issue ever made the ballot in such a conservative region indicates a gradual change in collective thinking for the American people. Also in November 2001, Maryland's Anti-Discrimination Act of 2001 went into effect. Maryland's gays and lesbians now have equal protection in housing, employment, and accommodations (American Civil Liberties Union Lesbian and Gay Rights Project, 2001).

What does this mean for nonprofit organizations? What does it mean for fundraisers?

By any other name

Before this chapter can proceed, one issue related to dealing with gay, lesbian, bisexual, and transgendered peoples must be addressed. On the surface this issue may appear minor. Still, it affects every level of communication related to the subject and the people. The issue is simply this: What does one call this particular population?

It is my observation that finding a name is a vital part of the metamorphosis from "victim" group to empowered people. For example, in the twentieth century as African Americans evolved from a state not far removed from slavery to holding an honored place in society, their name evolved: from *Negro*, to *colored*, to *black* or *African American*. And the evolution may well continue.

Gays, lesbians, bisexuals, and transgendered people face a particularly difficult challenge. Among publications serving the population itself, it is not unusual to see the abbreviations *glbt*, *GLBT*, *lgbt*, or *LGBT*. Although this practice would likely make the author of any language style manual run screaming into the streets, it makes practical a very basic concept in this population's metamorphosis to freedom. Many feel it is vital that there not be the practice of self-exclusion within the population itself. By listing the subpopulations of groups of alternative sexual orientations or gender identities (a separate but frequently related issue), one avoids the accidental exclusion of anyone.

In support of this concept, I wish to make clear that the concerns and issues of gay men, lesbians, bisexuals, and transgendered people are all to be considered in this chapter. For the sake of clarity and brevity, from this point forward, the simple term *gay* will be used to apply to all. This is by no means an intention to exclude any group who has faced or continues to face social and personal challenges because of nontraditional sexual orientation or gender identity.

Addressing the issue of name early in this chapter accomplishes another purpose as well. Fundraisers and the nonprofit organizations they serve will face unique challenges if they begin, for the first time, to address gay individuals and groups either as potential donors or as populations to be served. An awareness of the need to be conscious of something as simple as a name helps encourage the sensitivity needed to be successful in that effort.

And this means?

Let us go back to the original question, the one posed before the discussion of the issue of name. The times they are a-changin'— especially when it comes to gay issues. Gays have an increased visibility and gradual acceptance. So what does this mean for fundraisers and the organizations they serve?

It means many things. It means homosexuality is no longer, as it was in 1969, a subject discussed either in whispers or with shouts and rarely anything in between. It means that nonprofit organizations can no longer ignore the needs and wants of gay, lesbian, bisexual, or transgendered individuals—not if they see them as potential donors and not if they wish to effectively serve a sizable segment of the population. Many studies estimate at least 10 percent of the population is of an alternative sexual or gender orientation.

Those of nontraditional sexual orientation or gender identity are not a package of potential donors to be ignored. According to a recent survey conducted by Syracuse University, OpusComm Group, and GSociety, gay men and women spend about $514 billion a year (Syracuse University and OpusComm Group, 2001). The survey found that the 1999 U.S. median income of gay couples is $65,000, nearly 60 percent higher than the 1999 U.S. median income of $40,800. Nearly one-fifth of respondents to the survey reported a combined income of $100,000 or more, with 60 percent of male households and 46 percent of lesbian households having a combined income of over $60,000. "What we are finding in the study is that a good percentage of the gay and lesbian population are professionals who hold down well-paying jobs," says Jeffrey Garber, president of OpusComm Group and project leader for the survey (OpusComm Group, 2001). "It's a wake-up call to advertisers who are starting to follow the more traditionally gay-friendly marketing fray," says Cary Gilbert, vice president of GSociety (http://www.glcensus.org/downloads/GayJobs.htm).

Nonprofit opportunities

The wake-up call should not be limited to advertisers. The non-profit world has grown to accept the need for organizations to adjust to changing demographics. An effective awareness of demographic trends goes beyond the increase of ethnic and racial minorities—by 2010 one-third of all children will be black, Hispanic, or Asian (Nichols, 1990)—and has some rather unique applications when referring to the gay populations.

"Gay men and lesbians represent a huge potential market for charitable donations, but one that non-profit groups must nurture carefully if they hope to succeed at tapping it," said Arthur Makar, executive director of the American Lung Association of Queens, in Rego Park, New York, during the March 2001 annual meeting of the Association of Fundraising Professionals ("Solicited Advice," 2001).

From the present and looking back into the past, no one will ever have the data needed to effectively compare demographic changes for gays. It is only recently that studies and agencies have even dared to ask the questions. In 1990, for the first time, the U.S. Census Bureau included same-sex households in the categories of information collected. As of 2000, that remained the only data related to gay populations, and that one comparison proved amazing. Nationwide, in 2000 there was a 314 percent increase over the same-sex, unmarried partner households tallied in the 1990 census—601,209 households in 2000, compared with 145,130 in 1990 ("601,209 and Counting," 2001). The 2000 U.S. Census reported only twenty-two counties in the entire nation reporting no same-sex households.

"Imagine what the numbers would be if single gay, lesbian, bisexual and transgendered people were counted, if those in relationships but not living in the same household were counted, and if every same-sex couple felt comfortable disclosing their status on a government form," said Paula Ettelbrick, National Gay and Lesbian Task Force family policy director ("601,209 and Counting," 2001).

Demographics alone will not suffice if a fundraiser or organization wishes to understand gay donors and gay needs. There is a major psychological and social revolution happening for gays throughout the country and the world.

The 2001 Gay/Lesbian Consumer Online Census found that gays tend to identify more strongly with their sexual orientation than with their ethnic background. When asked if they identified more strongly with their ethnicity or sexual orientation, 85 percent of whites and 63 percent of African Americans said they perceived themselves first as gay (Syracuse University and OpusComm Group, 2001). Anytime an individual or a population feels asked or required to deny a part of self to achieve social acceptance, that issue becomes of vital importance. Gays are no exception.

Living in the confinement of control and persecution translated for many, if not most, into a life of secrecy and even shame. Although society has never been able to totally subjugate the homosexual, for many centuries it was a difficult existence. Life "in the closet" was not fun. This is important to remember as nonprofit organizations turn their attention to gays as potential donors. Gay individuals who have found freedom from the confinement of the closet will not likely accept having that portion of their self ignored, nor will they willingly accept either real or perceived prejudice.

Take, for example, the open recognition of gay heroes and victims of the September 11, 2001, terrorist attacks. Openly gay Mark Bingham is credited with helping fellow passengers thwart hijackers on United Airlines Flight 93 (Ritter and Kenworthy, 2001). Bingham helped in a passenger revolt that saved an unknown number of lives, an act that earned him consideration for the prestigious Medal of Freedom. When that airliner crashed in a Pennsylvania field instead of a populated area, Bingham and his copassengers literally went down fighting and became permanent inductees in the roster of American heroes.

In the not too distant past, Bingham's heroism would have been recognized but his gayness hidden. Some speculate that Bingham's experience as an openly gay man may have helped trigger the act of courage that thwarted at least one part of the coordinated terrorist attack. As many gays will assert, the decision not to hide one's sexuality helps create a life habit of standing against authority when necessary. This can be true when facing an employer, a public official, a landlord, or, as was quite possibly true in Bingham's case, terrorists with weapons.

Whether his sexuality and willingness to take a stand for gay issues helped Bingham perform an act of courage, there is no doubt that his partner and family displayed another kind of courage. By making public his sexuality, they proved the undeniable fact that gays can be heroes. This fact is nothing new. Gays are people, and, as with all populations, they include their fair share of heroes and villains. Throughout history, many famous people and acknowledged heroes have been gay (Lisker, 1969):

Short sample of gay public and historical figures
Alexander the Great
Susan B. Anthony
Sir Francis Bacon
Willa Cather
Amelia Earhart
Henry James
Margaret Mead
Harvey Milk
Lord Mountbatten
Florence Nightingale
Walt Whitman
Tennessee Williams

What is new is a willingness, and acceptance of the opportunity, to make public the sexual orientation of those gays who make valuable contributions to society. Nonprofits that wish to target gays as potential donors, must be aware of the importance of this empowerment to gays. Overlooking such basic issues can be deadly for organizations targeting gay populations.

When I was an officer in the U.S. Naval Reserve, I would occasionally assist in the coordination of military support for the funerals of veterans or service members. During the very powerful portion of graveside services in which an officer would present the flag to the spouse or family member of the deceased, I was occasionally plagued by a passing thought: If anything happened to me, who would get my flag?

This story illustrates an important factor for nonprofits seeking to address gays. The issue of sexuality is deeply personal for those who have faced and continue to face any form of prejudice or rejection related to their sexuality or gender identity. An organization with the courage to address the issue openly and publicly accept gay supporters will go a long way toward solidifying that support.

On the other hand, sensitivity to donor needs must also include an awareness of those who consider their sexuality a private matter or who, for various reasons, could be harmed by the disclosure of their sexuality. "Outing" (the making public of a gay's sexual orientation or gender identity) remains a sensitive issue that should be handled with care and awareness.

Longtime Association of Fundraising Professionals member and certified fundraising executive Marilyn Van Petten of Van Petten Resource Development in Amarillo, Texas, tells of a personal experience that made the unique needs of gays painfully real for her (interview, 2001). During a board training for a regional gay coalition on the Texas Panhandle, Van Petten presented "standard" information on how to process donor tracking and stewardship. This included acknowledging combined members of a household. "But we have people who could lose their jobs or be ousted by their families," an attendee observed.

Van Petten was sidetracked totally from the flow of her presentation and stood in silence processing what she had just been told. After the session she said that, in that moment, she finally understood what it could mean to be gay in relation to the realities of day-to-day life (interview, 2001). The experience helped her grow as a person and a professional, but it left unanswered questions (for her and many others) about how to incorporate the unique needs of gay donors into the fundraising world.

Arthur Makar addresses this critical question about acknowledging both members of a gay couple in donor recognition. He says that when donors are not listed together, "sometimes it's because it's a donor preference, but sometimes it's because the organization is a little squeamish about it" ("Solicited Advice," 2001). Makar's advice is simple: lose the squeamishness.

Planned giving wake-up call

Squeamishness control in relation to gay donors is especially valuable for fundraisers working in the field of planned giving. The for-profit world is already capitalizing on the first generation of "out" gays as they enter their retirement years. The needs of aging gays are addressed at newly developed retirement facilities such as the Palms of Manasota near St. Petersburg, Florida, and Rainbow Vision Properties in Santa Fe, New Mexico (Constable, 2002).

If one applies principles of societal forecasting, it is possible for businesses and nonprofit organizations to make early use of a major trend related to gays. As stated earlier, the Stonewall riots in New York in 1969 are known as the birthplace of the gay rights movement. Most of the leaders and participants in the effort to improve the visibility and social acceptance of gay populations were most likely in their thirties and forties at the start of this movement. Those courageous trendsetters are now in their sixties and seventies. This population is not only a valuable source of wisdom and history for nonprofits wishing to embrace gay groups and individuals; it also provides a resource of affluent individuals who are far more likely to give to organizations with the courage to "get over the squeamishness" concerning gays.

Retired gay community members, such as Hilda Rush, want to live in communities of people with similar backgrounds and life experiences. Rush, at the age of eighty-nine, refers to herself as Santa Fe's oldest living lesbian. She retired as a librarian for the Carnegie Endowment for International Peace in 1974. "I would prefer to live in a place that is exclusively for gays and lesbians," Rush said during an interview for the *Santa Fe New Mexican*. "Birds of a feather like to live together," she added (Constable, 2002).

For retirement facility developers, this awareness of and sensitivity to the desires of gays translates into business opportunities. Considering the higher median household income of gays— $65,000 for gay couples, in contrast to $40,800 for the general population (Syracuse University and OpusComm Group, 2001)—the potential benefits for nonprofit organizations are enormous, especially bearing in mind that gay couples are less likely to have children as a consideration in financial and estate planning.

Courage on the nonprofit front

Although there is certainly an appeal to the financial potential of tapping gays as potential donors, there is an even greater reason for nonprofit organizations to acknowledge gays. Fundraisers serve in a profession where basic terminology is tied to money. After all, the profession is composed of *fund*raisers who work for non*profits*. Sometimes it is all too easy to forget that financial efforts are rooted in the concept of philanthropy—the love of humanity. Philanthropy has a long and noble history of courage. After all, it is the nonprofit world that is society's "third sector."

The public sector (tax-funded entities) ensures that society stays up and running, but it is, to state the obvious, run by public officials. It is my observation that the nature of the political process makes it difficult for the public sector to address difficult issues until sufficient numbers of the population agree, thus allowing public officials to actually stay in office. By the time this is achieved, the issue is no longer difficult.

The private sector plays an equally important but entirely different role. Economic vitality remains dependent on businesses' ability to adapt to what makes enough people buy a product or service. For this reason the private sector must have a realistic approach to philanthropic efforts. If private enterprise pushes "comfort zones," uncomfortable consumers are likely to take their wallets elsewhere.

Then there is the third sector—the nonprofit world. It is that segment of society where philanthropy—the love of humanity—is at its best. The nonprofit world involves those individuals and organizations that dare dream of a better world and work to make that possible. Even before the term *nonprofit* came into use, the third sector was a vital part of a growing and vibrant society. Caring individuals formed organizations intended to address society's needs that were neither addressed by the public sector nor relevant to the economic environment of the private sector. One of the many complex roles of this third sector involves serving as a social conscience. For example, when the United States faced the complex issues surrounding slavery, organizations such as the American Anti-Slavery Society and the Unitarian Church enabled the nation to name and address difficult issues (Chittenden, 1973).

In many ways, the relevance is not so much which side of an issue any third sector organization supports. What is relevant is that an organization and the individuals who give that organization heart and substance have the strength and courage to face issues with dignity and respect for self and others.

Integration and acceptance of gay people remain a work in progress in one of the third sector's frontline efforts to nurture positive social evolution. The level of integrity vital to maintaining healthy nonprofit organizations requires individual and organizational soul-searching in dealing with such frontline efforts. Those third sector organizations that survive and thrive are those with the dynamic flexibility to address the evolving and, ideally, increasing ability for humanity to practice the highest ideals of philanthropy.

Being gay in the new millennium

Understanding the importance of welcoming gays as potential donors is just the beginning. Once an organization decides to "lose its squeamishness," as Makar recommends, there is still the question of where to go from there. It is one thing for an organization to decide to include gays as a part of inclusive policies, but it is another matter entirely to understand and serve this specific population.

Nonprofits face some special challenges when working with gay donors. On the one hand, an organization must show courage in openly acknowledging gays if it is to earn the respect and support of homosexual donors. On the other hand, an organization must be sensitive to those donors who still face some risk if their homosexuality is made public.

As stated earlier, organizational courage in facing frontline causes must involve soul-searching. Once an organization decides to include gays or gay causes, it would be naive to ignore the complexities of navigating in this subsociety. Let us look at two key issues affecting gays as individuals and as donors. These two issues are the heads and tails on the coin of life for gay individuals. They are gay pride and persecution.

Gay pride

Pride is like water. Most people take it for granted, but it becomes a subject of ultimate importance for those denied such a basic element. Any nonprofit organization wishing to serve gay individuals must recognize the importance of the expression of pride for members of the gay community. A booth at the local gay pride events or marching in the gay pride parade goes a long way toward earning donor loyalty. It can also go a long way toward earning an organization "brownie points" in the history of philanthropic courage.

Persecution

Daily life for gay individuals almost always includes some reminder of second-class citizenship. For example, committed gay couples routinely face the denial of the right to a legal marriage. Every time a couple seeks insurance through an employer and is denied, files a tax return, or even requests seating at an unwelcoming restaurant, there is a reminder that the world at large does not consider them "married." As difficult as that may be, it is one of the more benign forms of persecution faced by gays. There are still frequent verbal and physical attacks on gays by those who consider sexual orientation or gender identity to be justification for persecution.

Heads and tails

What do these two traits on the opposite ends of a continuum mean for nonprofit organizations? Basically, the balance between pride and persecution is a factor in almost every interaction relating to gays and gay issues. Like molecules in a gay universe, three molecules of pride to one molecule of persecution can produce one element. Four molecules of persecution to one molecule of pride produce another. An awareness of the mix and proportions can help a nonprofit organization adapt as needed according to the situation or donor. To fully understand this dilemma, it may help to step back and look at what life is like for a few gay individuals. (Do not forget that in this chapter *gay* is being used as an all-inclusive term for those of nontraditional sexual orientation or gender identity.)

Take, for example, Jonathan. Here is an accomplished professional with a successful business. He and his partner are leaders in both the community at large and in the gay organizations of their city. They walk a constant tightrope of being "out" and "closeted" because of conflicting desires to improve the status of gays in general and to continue functioning effectively as mainstream leaders in a conservative city. They give regularly to gay organizations, educational institutions, their church, and other organizations and causes that share their philosophies of life and philanthropy.

Then there is Sandra. As an official with one of the largest gay organizations in the country, she lives, breathes, and sleeps gay issues and gay causes. If she gives to an organization and that organization fails to include her partner in donor recognition efforts, she is likely to show up on their doorstep demanding to know why.

Oh yes, do not forget Paula. For the past twenty years, she has been a successful and respected teacher in a small, rural community. She and her partner live quiet lives, accepted by their neighbors because of their kindness and willingness to serve. In something of a throwback to days gone by, no one questions the lives of these two longtime "roommates." They are simply a part of the community, accepted as individuals. They give to their community through the service organizations in which they volunteer and participate. For them it is simply a part of being good neighbors.

What about Joanna? After many years living in a body that did not feel like her own, she underwent the costly and difficult physical and mental process of transformation from the life of a man to that of a woman. After the change was complete, she attempted to return to the conservative region that was her home, but moved back to a larger city shortly after someone fired four shotgun blasts through her bedroom window. Now she lives happily as part of a larger community where she knows and associates with other transsexuals who understand and share her life experience. She gives quietly, including discrete donations to organizations back in the conservative city that will always be the home of her heart.

What do all of these individuals have in common, besides being gay? First, they are fictional, but each is based on traits and experiences from actual people. Second, they are all donors. Looking at these examples, anyone can see that there is no one-size-fits-all approach to the care and nurturing of gay donors. So how does a nonprofit organization deal effectively with gay donors and gay clients?

Getting from point A to point B

If the decision to solicit gay donors is point A and developing quality long-term relationships with gay donors is point B, nonprofits may face occasionally bumpy and largely uncharted territory on the journey between those two points. Even those nonprofit organizations that specifically serve gay populations face special challenges in donor stewardship. One specific example is donor recognition. Although making public a person's sexuality is not the issue it once was, when seeking sponsors for gay events, an organization cannot safely assume that a donor wishes to be listed as a sponsor. Before making a name public, an organization must know the background and possible implications for a donor. Another example is the ethical dilemma some gay organizations face when recruiting leadership. Sometimes the most qualified individuals still have areas in which their private lives remain "closeted." I have heard and participated in heated debates concerning whether or not gay leaders have a moral obligation to be open about their sexuality.

As with any soul-searching effort, whether by an individual or an organization, the answers come one question at a time. Each decision is a part of the evolution of empowerment for gay communities, organizations, and people.

If the handling of gay donors is complex for gay organizations, what is it like for mainstream organizations as they take that courageous step to embrace gays as donors and clients? One of the first steps in addressing gays, or any diverse population, is actual interaction with the community. When learning about a new group or earning trust, there is no substitute for presence.

The central leadership of the Association of Fundraising Professionals (AFP) provided an outstanding example of this principle during the 2001 AFP international conference in San Diego, California. Each year the Gill Foundation of Denver, Colorado, one of the largest supporters of gay issues and organizations, sponsors a number of gays in attending the AFP conference. Gill's efforts include a special reception not only for their sponsored participants but also for other gay attendees and friends and supporters of gays and their organizations. When the officers from AFP's international board made an appearance at that reception, their presence proved beyond a doubt AFP's open inclusion of gays and their organizations.

There is a simple truth that many, if not most, mainstream organizations overlook when attempting outreach to diverse groups. Welcoming someone to a new environment involves more than opening the doors. An open door is worth little without an extended hand, especially if "outsiders" have a real or perceived reason to believe they were once unwelcome.

If an organization wants to welcome gays, it must send individuals to interact with the community. After all, individuals, not organizations, earn trust, and as any fundraiser should know, giving is about trust. Improving these communication channels can also help in maneuvering in the potential "minefield" of donor recognition for gays. Basically, if one does not know what to do, ask. It is another example of the need to lose the squeamishness.

As an increasing number of nonprofit organizations manage to overcome this squeamishness and acknowledge and expand their service to gay populations, something happens that is so obvious it can be overlooked. Is it not obvious that the philanthropic world should include gays in its efforts to express basic "love of humanity"? After all, gays are and always have been a part of humanity.

References

American Civil Liberties Union Lesbian and Gay Rights Project. "Maryland Gay Rights Law Takes Effect; Referendum 'Forever' Dead." *News from the ACLU Lesbian and Gay Rights Project,* Nov. 21, 2001.

Chittenden, E. *Profiles in Black and White: Stories of Men and Women Who Fought Against Slavery.* New York: Scribner, 1973.

Constable, A. "Gay and Lesbian Retirement Communities Planned for Santa Fe." *Santa Fe New Mexican,* Jan. 20, 2002, p. B1.

Lisker, J. "Homo Nest Raided, Queen Bees Are Stinging Mad." *New York Daily News,* July 6, 1969, pp. 1–4.

Nichols, J. E. *Changing Demographics.* Chicago: Bonus Books, 1990.

OpusComm Group. "Computer Technology and Education Lead Gay/Lesbian Jobs, Major Survey Finds." Press release, Nov. 11, 2001.

"Rights Advocates Hail Important Election Victories." *Data Lounge.* [http://www.datalounge.com]. Nov. 25, 2001.

Ritter, J., and Kenworthy, T. "Passengers Likely Halted Attack on D.C." *USA Today,* Oct. 2, 2001.

"601,209 and Counting: Census Figures on Same-Sex Unmarried Partner Households Released for All 50 States." *NGLTF News and Views.* [http://www.ngltf.org]. Aug. 22, 2001.

"Solicited Advice." *Chronicle of Philanthropy,* Mar. 22, 2001, p. 24.

Syracuse University and OpusComm Group. "2001 Gay/Lesbian Consumer Online Census." [http://www.glcensus.org]. 2001.

KAY C. PECK *is director of development for the National Institute for Native Leadership in Albuquerque, New Mexico. She is a founding member of OUTstanding Amarillo, the gay, lesbian, bisexual, and transgendered organization in Amarillo, Texas.*

Managing diversity has grown beyond affirmative action, with its focus on counting groups and ensuring participation, to focus on creating a culture in which diverse individuals use different perspectives to meet an organization's mission. A communication perspective can help us create an organizational culture that welcomes diversity.

3

Using a communication perspective to manage diversity in the development office

William F. Bartolini

HAVING A DIVERSE STAFF enthusiastically working together to meet the organization's objectives is a noble and appropriate goal. But when people of different backgrounds come together—whether staff, volunteers, or donors—misunderstandings and conflicts are likely to arise. How does the development office manager provide leadership in this situation, developing a cohesive group of individuals who celebrate their differences yet work together to reach common goals?

The purpose of this chapter is to address these issues by developing a working definition of diversity and what it means to "manage diversity," discussing from a communication perspective how people tend to interact with diverse groups of people, and exploring the implications for managing diversity in the development office.

NEW DIRECTIONS FOR PHILANTHROPIC FUNDRAISING, NO. 34, WINTER 2001 © WILEY PERIODICALS, INC.

Understanding the complexity of diversity

When they think of diversity, most people call to mind categories of individuals such as people of a certain race, gender, or age. Even today, many people believe that diversity just means including people of different races in our workplaces. Perhaps this is an outgrowth of early laws and civil rights movements in the United States. Political initiatives like affirmative action and equal opportunity were meant to ensure equal access by counting and protecting "classes" of people. It should be noted, however, that providing equity and embracing diversity are different processes. Equity involves treating everyone the same, in "a manner that respects their intrinsic worth and dignity" (Fischer, 1997, p. 66). Diversity, on the other hand, is valuing the differences and the unique contributions people can bring to the project at hand (Kandola and Fullerton, 1994).

Although classifying individuals by categories—a *social category approach* to diversity—has been useful to understanding diversity, some organizations have found it more beneficial to view diversity by its relevance to organizational performance (Schneider and Northcraft, 1999). Managers may find this approach to diversity, sometimes called a *functional category approach*, helpful in ensuring they have employees who bring to the organization different knowledge, skills, abilities, values, beliefs, or attitudes (McGrath, Berdahl, and Arrow, 1995; Schneider and Northcraft, 1999). Still others have found it helpful to obtain a balance of how people make decisions (based on their thoughts or feelings), how they gather information (through the five senses or relying on the "sixth sense," intuition), and what energizes their world (whether they are extroverted or introverted). A personality assessment, such as the Myers-Briggs Type Indicator (Hirsch and Kummerow, 1990), can help guide functional category diversity.

The categorical logic has been extended by many, including the Association of Fundraising Professionals (1995) in its *Building a High Performing Diverse Chapter*, to suggest that an organization should ensure its board of trustees represents diverse backgrounds (Kandola and Fullerton, 1996). Many organizations attempt to achieve a diversity of occupations, income levels, backgrounds, and experiences among the board members. For instance, some consider it important to achieve a balance based on geographical representation, profession, or relationship to the organization (for example, client, supplier, or donor).

Some diversity may be observable. For instance, often it is possible to observe someone's race. But a categorical difference may not be obvious immediately and thus may be considered "hidden" (Hecht and Faulkner, 2000). For example, one's religion or sexual orientation is not always readily observed and may be known only through self-revelation by the individual.

Further, categorization may be a function either of others or of oneself. That is, an observer may decide another individual belongs in a particular category. For instance, one may decide you "look" Hispanic and place you in that category, whether the assumption is correct or not. But a person also may identify with a category and thus self-categorize with a group (Gudykunst and Ting-Toomey, 1990). One may not be overtly Catholic, gay, or Hispanic but may feel an affinity for, and thus self-identify with, the particular group.

In part because of self-categorization, some researchers have suggested considering diversity as an element of an individual's personal identity, not as group state (Hecht and Faulkner, 2000; Gudykunst and Ting-Toomey, 1990). This pluralistic model, or *identity approach*, suggests *people* embody their diversity qualities. Diversity, in this view, is an internal function of identity that may or may not be readily observable. Thus an African American, a Jew, or a lesbian may or may not choose to identify with the source of his or her diversity at any particular moment. All may at one moment assimilate in thought and action with the majority or, at another time, diverge from the majority and self-identify with the source of their diversity. Further, when it is in an individual's self-interest, the individual may decide to make the diversity evident; when it may cause harm, the individual may hide the identification (Hraba and Hoiberg, 1983; Hecht and Faulkner, 2000).

The identity approach suggests diversity, like culture, is a psychological state that is part of "a broader self-management and self-presentation process" (Gudykunst and Ting-Toomey, 1990, p. 311).

An individual, in this view, manages and presents self-identity through communication (Hecht and Faulkner, 2000).

Thus diverse identity includes how the individual thinks about self as an independent being in relation to others, as part of a shared group identity—and how those thoughts of identity are expressed through action. Recognizing how diversity can be represented in various aspects of identity can be useful when using a communication perspective to manage and facilitate efforts in the development office.

Thus, although counting individuals based on a social or functional category may ensure representation of diverse individuals, it does not ensure that difference is welcomed, encouraged, and accepted or that the organization uses diverse perspectives to excel at its work. Successful leaders not only must ensure a diverse group of employees is gathered together but also must manage the work setting to ensure diversity is working on behalf of the institution's mission. In short, successful leaders must "manage diversity" in the development office.

What is managing diversity?

Managing diversity is concerned with recognizing difference, facilitating communication, and developing a culture that welcomes and embraces the individual contributions people with differing perspectives can bring to the organization. For the United States this is a significant paradigm shift away from affirmative action or equal opportunity, which are concerned with counting categories of individuals, making sure they have equal opportunities, and seeing that all are represented. Ensuring that all groups have access and opportunities is important, but *managing diversity shifts the focus away from counting groups to ensuring participation* (Kandola and Fullerton, 1994).

Managing diversity is concerned with individuals (not groups)—and with embracing their differences and facilitating their participation—for the mutual benefit of those involved and the organization (Lawthom, 2000). Kandola and Fullerton (1996,

p. 288), who bring a European perspective to the issue, succinctly conceptualize managing diversity by saying, "The basic concept of managing diversity accepts that the workforce consists of a diverse population of people. The diversity consists of visible and non-visible differences, which will include factors such as sex, age, background, race, disability, personality, work style. It is founded on the premise that harnessing these differences will create a productive environment in which everybody feels valued, where their talents are being fully utilized and in which organizational goals are met." In short, managing diversity focuses on facilitating the contributions of all employees, "even white middle-class males" (Kandola and Fullerton, 1996, p. 288).

What are the benefits of diversity in the development office?

Engaging a functionally and categorically diverse staff can provide distinct benefits to the organization. These benefits are not achieved without challenge and, in some cases, not without experiencing short-term costs (Schneider and Northcraft, 1999). Some research has indicated, for instance, that homogeneous groups accomplish more in the short term. In the long term, however, a diverse group provides more benefits to the organization (Lawthom, 2000). A brief overview of those benefits follows.

Better decision making

Diversity among employees provides more opportunities to identify problems, recognize important information, and discover potential solutions. However, success comes not from having more input but from the variety of backgrounds and perspectives that are brought to bear on the issue at hand (Kandola and Fullerton, 1994).

Better organizational culture and more innovation

Studies have shown that organizations comprising diverse populations are more innovative, have a greater sense of renewal, and express more creativity (Schneider and Northcraft, 1999). A diverse staff who have varied external networks have the potential to bring fresh new ideas to the development office, ideas that are likely to help raise much-needed resources. The diverse staff also is likely to be motivated to succeed. Because there is a tendency to assume that individuals from the minority group are less qualified to accomplish the work, many diverse individuals work harder to demonstrate competence (Shallenberger, 1996; Steele and Aronson, 1995).

Improved recruitment and retention

The diverse organization has an easier time recruiting qualified employees from a diverse population pool (Lawthom, 2000). Although there may be initial challenges and short-term costs associated with diversity initiatives (Schneider and Northcraft, 1999), in the long term, many organizations report fewer people leave and seek other employment, thus improving retention rates (Kandola and Fullerton, 1994).

Improved image with minority groups

Diverse employees who enjoy working in the development office are likely to act as organizational ambassadors and speak positively about the organization to those in their sphere of influence (Lawthom, 2000). Employees' minority-based connections can be just as helpful as what is commonly called the "old boys' network."

In summary, having a group of employees with a wide variety of backgrounds, ethnicities, cultures, orientations, and approaches to life can provide a variety of benefits to the organization. However, managing a development office of diverse employees also can be a challenge. A communication perspective can assist in managing diversity.

Using a communication perspective to manage diversity

Communication can be difficult, whether one is attempting to communicate with a significant other, friend, boss, or coworker.

The difficulty of communicating can be exacerbated when diverse people come together. For instance, "yes" means agreement and even can be a verbal contract to many North Americans. To a Chinese individual, however, "yes" has multiple levels of meaning and may just indicate "I'm listening" or "that's possible" (Gao, 1998, p. 163). One study found that highly educated communicators of the same culture understand only 75 percent of the intended message, whereas highly educated listeners from differing cultures understand only 50 percent of the conveyed information (Li, 1999). Consider, for instance, how often have you heard something like "I'm sorry, we apparently misunderstood each other" or "What we had here was a failure to communicate!"

It seems like there never can be enough communication, but what really is missing is *mindful* communication. Because communication is ubiquitous—that is, it is omnipresent and people are constantly doing it—we often communicate automatically, as if we were performing habitually and no longer needed to think about what we are doing. Mindful communication means we carefully analyze the communication that comes to us and are thoughtful about our responses so we can effectively understand what others are trying to say and convey our interests in a way that increases the probability that we will be understood (Gudykunst, 1998). In managing diversity, communicating mindfully can be especially useful. (This will be discussed in greater detail shortly.)

What follows are some important communication concepts—generally drawn from an interpersonal perspective—that are applicable to managing diverse development offices, focusing on the larger issues involved. Key communication concepts will be presented, followed by a discussion of their practical application to managing the development office.

Communication patterns

Many people have been taught that communication involves someone sending a message, another person receiving and interpreting the message, and providing feedback to the original sender. Effective communication—which occurs when the sent message and feedback are properly interpreted—requires that individuals "achieve coordination by managing the ways messages take on meaning" (Cronen, Pearce, and Harris, 1982, p. 68). Conceptualized as the *coordinated management of meaning*, communication is a process "in which each person interprets and responds to the acts of another, monitors the sequence, and compares it to his or her desires and expectations" (Cronen, Pearce, and Harris, 1982, p. 68).

Each individual has developed a variety of rules, or schema, that guide the interpretation of communication. In essence, the schema provide a framework people use to make sense of the world and to judge whether something is appropriate or inappropriate, liked or disliked. Based on their schema, people view the world and make judgments about what others are saying, what their motives are, and whether their actions are important. This is not to say that one person's schema is right or wrong, but that communicators need to be aware of their schema and ready to put them aside when communicating with others from different backgrounds.

Stereotypes as a schema

One schema that is often used is stereotypes, especially when people do not have enough information to make appropriate judgments (Gudykunst and Nishida, 2001). Stereotypes can be useful when used in a disciplined fashion (Adler, 1996). They are not good or bad; they just are. How they are used determines their value. According to Adler, stereotypes can be helpful when they are

- *Consciously held.* For the stereotype to be helpful, the person using the stereotype must be aware that it is being used to describe a group's qualities rather than the qualities of an individual.
- *Descriptive rather than evaluative.* The stereotype should be used to describe how the people of a group probably would react to communication, so as to facilitate interaction, not to provide judgments of the people as good or bad.
- *Accurate.* The stereotype should indeed describe the norm of the particular group.

- *The first best guess.* Stereotypes are most helpful when they provide a baseline of information from which to start the conversation, especially in initial interactions.
- *Modified.* Stereotypes should be updated to provide more accurate information based on one's experience with the members of the group.

Because they influence the way information is processed, stereotypes must be used mindfully. For instance, people tend to remember more favorable information about their own groups but more easily remember unfavorable information about stereotyped groups (Gudykunst, 1987). Similarly, people see greater differences among members of their own groups but see less difference among stereotyped groups (Park and Judd, 1990). This is the reason behind the offensive statement "They all look alike," which is sometimes said of unfamiliar cultures. In reality, "they" all look very different and have many individualizing qualities. However, the person making the statement sees difference in his or her own culture but has not learned to differentiate the individuals in the unfamiliar culture.

People also use stereotypes to create behavioral expectations for the target of the stereotype and themselves. For instance, people generally confirm expectations by looking for information that fits the stereotype they hold (Gudykunst, 1987). The targets of the stereotype can overcompensate and become overachievers (Shallenberger, 1996) or may be so affected by the stereotype that they will behave in a way to confirm it. In one classic research study, for example, a group of individuals were told that their race was not as intelligent as the majority group and that they were not expected to do as well on the achievement tests because of it. The minority group confirmed the stereotype by not doing as well, when in fact they were just as intelligent (Steele and Aronson, 1995). In summary, stereotypes can be misused and can have negative effects on communication. However, used mindfully, stereotypes can be useful.

Stereotypes are just one kind of schema people use to judge the world and determine appropriateness. Everyone has beliefs, habits, and ways of doing things that are central to their cultural and ethnic background. In that sense, all people—not just "others"—are ethnocentric (Lawthom, 2000).

Impact of diversity on communication

Earlier it was noted that individuals must have a common interpretation to successfully communicate. Yet because diverse individuals bring their unique backgrounds to their interpretations, communication challenges exist when people with different experiences come together in the development office. Having a basic understanding of individuals' cultural backgrounds and the perspectives they bring to the conversation can greatly enhance communication understanding.

For our purposes here, culture is considered a common group affiliation as it is personally expressed. When people develop a logic, or symbolic structure, in their minds and then communicate around that concept, they accept and become part of that culture. Individuals also learn values that guide their behavior as they are socialized into a culture (Gudykunst and Ting-Toomey, 1990). Again, through this socialization, people create schema that guide their communication and actions.

In his seminal work spanning several decades, Hofstede (1991, 1996) identified four basic dimensions of national cultures that affect communication. These dimensions, which are dichotomous continuums measuring some of the value orientations people bring to the communication situation, include (1) individualism versus collectivism, (2) large or small power distance, (3) strong or weak uncertainty avoidance, and (4) masculinity versus femininity. The dimension that has generated the most profitable communication research relates to a person's individualism versus collectivism.

Those who have an *individualistic* frame of reference view the self as a unique combination of "preferences, traits, abilities, motives, values, and rights" (Kim, Shin, and Cai, 1998, p. 49). They take action based on these internal attributes. In individualistic cultures people often are socialized to meet their personal needs before helping others meet their needs and to see themselves as independent of collectives. In terms of their communication style, the individualists often express emotion, speak longer and louder, and believe that it is important to be direct (Gudykunst, Matsumoto, Ting-Toomey, and Nishida, 1996).

In contrast, individuals with a *collectivistic* orientation consider themselves more strongly linked to a larger group, such as the family, culture, coworkers, or nation. They see themselves "not as an independent entity separate from the collective, but instead as a priori fundamentally interdependent with others" (Kim, Shin, and Cai, 1998, p. 49). In essence, their self-concept is based on their role in the group, and they are more likely to meet the group's goals before their own. In terms of communication style, the collectivist often believes it is important to fit in, act appropriately, and rely on hints and indirect statements. What is *not* said may be just as important as what is said; communication may be based on assuming people know certain information, rules, or roles, so mentioning them is not appropriate.

Hofstede (1991) rated the cultures of fifty countries around the world on the individualist-collectivist orientation. The United States received the highest individualistic score. Many European nations, such as Great Britain, France, Sweden, and Belgium, also were found to be individualistic, as were Australia and Canada. People from these countries are likely to value individual initiative, speak directly, and handle conflicts confrontationally as they arise (Ting-Toomey and others, 2000). Generally, Asian countries (such as Singapore, Taiwan, Thailand, Indonesia, and Pakistan), Latin countries (such as Colombia, Guatemala, Mexico, Peru, Venezuela, Spain, and Portugal), and Arab countries (such as Egypt, Lebanon, Libya, Kuwait, Iraq, and Saudi Arabia) were found to be collectivistic (for a detailed and accessible review of Arab cultural communication patterns, see Feghali, 1997). People from these cultures are more likely to value the good of the group over personal gain, prefer indirect statements, and avoid or use others to help resolve conflict (Ting-Toomey and others, 2000). As with all classifications, it must be noted that there will be individualists in collectivistic societies and collectivists in individualistic cultures. However, the general findings may help development office leaders understand others' schema and in the process manage diversity by facilitating communication.

Hofstede's (1991, 1996) individualist-collectivist dimension has received the most attention, but the other three dimensions have value in understanding the schema people use to conceptualize themselves and the world. The second of the four dimensions, *power distance*, refers to how the culture approaches power differences that are a natural part of life. Some people, having a higher tolerance for inequity and accepting it as part of life, are likely to be more mindful of authority, whereas others who strive for equity are more likely to question authority.

For the development office this means the manager should be aware of differences in how people approach power. Some are going to follow the boss's established direction and get along even at the risk of not fulfilling the organization's mission. Others will approach power more critically, questioning the direction and seeking to influence decisions. These two approaches are not right or wrong; they just are. Leadership in the development office requires a recognition of these differences and an adjustment in how one approaches employees of differing perspectives.

The other two dimensions Hofstede (1991, 1996) identified include uncertainty avoidance and masculinity versus femininity. *Uncertainty avoidance* refers to the fact that people are constrained by time and that the future is uncertain. Some people are socialized to accept the uncertainty of the future and not be upset by it. These people will "take risks rather easily. They will not work as hard. They will be relatively tolerant of behavior and opinions different from their own because they do not feel threatened by them" (Hofstede, 1996, p. 253). These individuals have low uncertainty avoidance and are likely to be more open to communication about new initiatives that have some inherent risk. In contrast, people of high uncertainty avoidance feel greater anxiety over the unknown future. These individual may try to take whatever actions they can to "beat the future," and their anxiety may manifest itself in greater "nervousness, emotionality, and aggressiveness" (Hofstede, 1996, p. 253). Coming from a strong uncertainty avoidance perspective, these individuals often look for absolute truths and are less likely to welcome communication about new projects. Routine, rules, and policies can be comforting to these individuals.

In the final dimension, Hofstede (1991, 1996) identified cultures on a continuum of *masculinity-femininity*. Highly masculine-oriented cultures place "values on things, money, and assertiveness" (Gudykunst, 1987, p. 855). Successful communication with these individuals may relate to competition, the importance of achieving goals, and the importance of winning for the team. In contrast, feminine-oriented cultures place value on "people, quality of life, and nurturance" (Gudykunst, 1987, p. 855). Communication that appeals to working as a team and improving the life of others yet recognizes the contribution of the individual is likely to be more appealing to those who approach communication from a feminine orientation.

This chapter will now examine how individuals are likely to react when encountering difference—and how managing diversity can help people manage these encounters.

Interactions with dissimilar others: Managing anxiety and uncertainty

People seek similarity and a sense of affinity in initial meetings (Bell and Daly, 1984; Martin and Rubin, 1998). Often, in the United States, rituals such as shaking hands and asking "How are you?" are used to establish the similarity and affinity that are necessary before individuals risk more serious communication. In India people place their hands in a praying position and give a slight bow, called a *namaste*. In Thailand a similar gesture called the *wai* is given as a respectful greeting. In New Zealand the Maori people rub noses. Some Tibetan tribesman stick out their tongues. Many Asians give a slight bow. And in many Latin American countries, people engage in an *abrazo*, or embrace, sometimes with "hearty claps on the back" (Axtell, 1998, p. 21).

When people meet strangers, they may expand their rituals to include a repertoire of information-seeking behaviors as a way of learning more about the other person and seeking affinity (Martin and Rubin, 1998). For instance, they may ask questions (interrogation), share some personal information about themselves in response to shared information (self-disclosure), evaluate the other person's trustworthiness or honesty (deception detection), or make comparisons to judge how "normal" the other person is (deviation testing) (Berger and Calabrese, 1975). These actions are all meant to increase the amount of information individuals have about the other person and increase their comfort level.

When encountering unfamiliar communication situations—including meeting individuals of different cultures—people are likely to experience discomfort in two dimensions: anxiety and uncertainty (Gudykunst and Nishida, 1984). *Anxiety* is the emotional reaction. It is the tension, apprehension, and uneasy feelings one has in dealing with other cultures. *Uncertainty* is the cognitive reaction and refers to the thoughts people have about how to best handle the situation, the attributions that are made about why someone is behaving in a certain way, and the predictions that are made about another's behavior. Development professionals managing a diverse office staff may need to facilitate the staff's understanding of these feelings and thoughts and help them be mindful in managing their uncertainty. Mindfulness involves creating more distinctions, being open to new information, and recognizing there may be "more than one perspective that can be used to understand or explain [people's] interactions" (Gudykunst, 1998, p. 234).

When people feel excessive anxiety, their feelings can get in the way of communicating effectively. Anxious individuals tend to communicate mindlessly, without thinking, and make judgments based on their own cultural schema rather than taking the other person's frame of reference into consideration (Gudykunst, 1998). At these times people often will rely on stereotypes, making judgments based on groups of individuals rather than based on the individual (Gudykunst and Nishida, 2001). Development office leadership can help people relax during communication, allowing them to reduce anxiety and think more clearly about how to react.

Just as anxiety represents the emotional dimension of communicating with diverse individuals, uncertainty reflects the cognitive one. When people are unsure of the communication situation or the other person's attitudes, feelings, or potential reactions (Gudykunst and Nishida, 2001), their thoughts reflect their uncertainty, and they are more likely to rely on stereotypes for decision making (Armstrong and Kaplowitz, 2001). In these situations people also are more likely to attribute the actions of others to their failings rather than to the situation. In contrast, people are likely to attribute their own failings to the situation at hand, not to their own shortcomings (Heider, 1958; for an accessible review of Heider's work, see Fiske and Taylor, 1991). However, when people have certainty in the communication situation, they feel confident they can predict the other person's behavior and meaning—and communication is more effective. By focusing on the cultural differences affecting the other person's communication, individuals can be mindful and reduce the uncertainty. How this can be done is reflected in the next section on the implications for managing diversity.

Implications for managing diversity in the development office

This chapter proposes that diversity can best be managed in the development office using an individual-focused, interpersonal communication perspective. Although most of the examples presented are about managing diversity in the office, many of the principles are applicable to engaging volunteers and donors. The information is organized around three guiding steps: setting the stage for success, communicating to facilitate understanding, and monitoring success.

Step 1: Set the stage for success

Setting the stage for success includes making sure you and your staff are ready to accept diversity as important to the success of the organization.

Assume we are all diverse. People bring different cultures, experiences, and perspectives to the development office regardless of whether they are in the majority or nonmajority group. These differences are an integral part of one's identity and may or may not be observable. We are all diverse. If we assume just *others* are different or diverse—such as just those who are in the minority race, who have a different sexual orientation, who originated in a different country, or who like to wear purple hair—then we assume *we* are "normal" and that others are not. These attitudes continue to create a system of inequality. Fischer (1997, p. 70) noted that "until those who consider themselves 'normal' replace that mentality with the clear understanding that their perspective is but one among many, the schema for stigma remains." In short, we must begin with the understanding that we are all diverse.

Evaluate your own assumptions, and help others examine theirs. As noted earlier, people use schema to judge the meaning behind what others are saying or doing, the way to react in a certain situation, and the behavior that is appropriate in a given context. Schema are developed as an individual is socialized into a culture and are the result of experiences. Managers often are part of the majority, or in-group, and may not recognize that others do not share their assumptions. Thus individuals from different backgrounds may not share the same mode of operating. Recall that when individuals do not have enough information, they rely on stereotypes. The use of stereotypes can be helpful when they are consciously held, nonjudgmental, accurate, and revised when new information becomes available. Consider, however, that several studies have shown that white managers are presumed competent unless proven otherwise, whereas managers who are not part of the majority group—such as women and minorities—are presumed to be less competent until they have proved themselves (Lawthom, 2000). The successful manager is a builder of people, gives people the benefit of the doubt, and provides opportunities for people to prove themselves.

Assess where you and your staff are in terms of experience with diversity. Successful communication is built on understanding the other person's schema, interpreting the other person's messages, and engaging in mindful communication. Learning how to handle this process takes conscious practice. It follows, then, that exposure to diversity can help the development office staff develop the skills necessary. In short, "as one's *experience of cultural difference* becomes more complex and sophisticated, one's competence in intercultural relations increases" (Hammer and Bennett, 2001, p. 4).

Under this developmental view of diversity, individuals move along a continuum as they gain more sophistication in dealing with difference. People progress through three stages while in an *ethnocentric* orientation and then continue through three stages after developing an *ethnorelative* orientation. The ethnocentric orientation suggests "one's own culture is experienced as central to reality in some way" (Hammer and Bennett, 2001, p. 6). When in this orientation, individuals move through the stages of *denial*, *defense*, and *minimization*. *Denial* is the beginning stage, in which individuals only have experience with their own personal culture. People in denial "generally are disinterested in cultural difference when it is brought to their attention" (p. 6). *Defense* indicates people have some experience with other cultures and are threatened by them. At this stage people may have developed schema in which "the world is organized into 'us and them,' where one's own culture is superior and other cultures are inferior" (p. 6). *Minimization* suggests people recognize that individuals from other cultures have similar experiences, although application of "'universal absolutes' obscure[s] deep cultural differences, [so] other cultures may be trivialized or romanticized" (p. 7).

After progressing through the three states in the ethnocentric orientation, individuals exposed to diversity can progress through the three stages of the ethnorelative orientation: *acceptance*, *adaptation*, and *integration*. The ethnorelative orientation suggests "one's own culture is experienced in context of the other cultures" (Hammer and Bennett, 2001, p. 7). *Acceptance* is the stage in which people view their own culture as just one of many equally valid approaches. Acceptance is followed by *adaptation*, in which individuals not only see other cultures as equally valid but also incorporate appealing elements into their own view, including taking the perspective of the other culture. Finally, people who have been exposed to other cultures and have incorporated their experiences into their frames of reference achieve *integration*, which refers to a sense of self that includes "the movement in and out of different cultural worldviews" (p. 8).

Development office leadership can assess the level of the staff's experience with diversity and whether the staff has integrated that experience into their perspectives of self and the world. For instance, people who are in the ethnocentric orientation may be "*avoiding cultural difference*, either by denying its existence, by raising defenses against it, or by minimizing its importance" (Hammer and Bennett, 2001, p. 9). In contrast, those who are in the ethnorelative orientation are likely to be "*seeking cultural difference*, either by accepting its importance, by adapting perspective to take it into account, or by integrating the whole concept into a definition of identity" (p. 9). By understanding how the staff has moved along the continuum, development office leadership can plan more learning experiences for the staff and help them to integrate a diverse view in their perspectives.

Step 2: Communicate to facilitate understanding

Communicating to facilitate understanding involves discussing diversity in a way that will overcome the anxiety and uncertainty that occur when individuals encounter difference (Gudykunst, 1998). The following sections discuss five specific techniques useful for building a unified but diverse staff.

Talk about diversity. Often people are afraid of not being politically correct or of saying the wrong things. Subjects are avoided, especially when people know they are problematic. In the United States this has led to the metaphor of an "elephant in the living room" that no one is talking about. In contrast to this behavior, however, people can best work together to achieve common goals when there is communication and understanding. Development office leadership must put the fear of offending aside and begin discussing differences openly, in a supportive atmosphere. When we do so, we gain understanding, reduce tensions, and enhance organizational effectiveness.

Often those in the nonmajority group feel subordinate and powerless when they are silent about the differences. These feelings can be exacerbated if individuals strongly relate their diversity to their identity. Speaking about difference—the elephant in the living room—can empower individuals and increase self-esteem. Open discussions can empower the nonmajority group by communicating that there is no shame in being different and that the difference does not impede the capability to accomplish work. Open communication about difference has been associated with higher levels of self-esteem in the nonmajority group (Shallenberger, 1996).

Of course, individuals should not be required or forced to discuss their differences, especially if the source of the diversity is not readily apparent. Employees should not be "outed" or the source of their diversity revealed by others. Rather, recognize that individuals make personal decisions to discuss their diversity after considering the impact of the revelation on their self-image and on their relationship with others (Hecht and Faulkner, 2000). Thus managers should create an atmosphere where self-disclosure of diversity is appropriate and welcomed—and where it is "safe" to disclose and not suffer emotional repercussions.

Facilitate dialogue to establish sameness. Recall that people are more comfortable communicating when they perceive some affinity or commonality with others (Bell and Daly, 1984; Martin and Rubin, 1998). In addition, people can become anxious and experience uncertainty when they are faced with new situations and unable to predict others' reactions (Gudykunst, 1987). Thus a sense of sameness or being part of the in-group often is present before meaningful dialogue occurs. Disclosing personal information can help create the sense of trust and affinity necessary for communication. In fact, those who self-disclose information through a variety of tactics have been shown to be more competent at creating affinity (Rubin, Rubin, and Martin, 1993).

Therefore the development office manager should help people feel a sense of comfort in commonality. Employees could be asked to share experiences around similar or universal issues as a way to develop a common baseline. Perhaps diverse employees could be asked to share stories about meetings with donors that had disappointing or exhilarating outcomes, or explore the commonality of issues around parenting, raising children, or dealing with aging parents. In the process, help others learn to be sensitive, and listen closely to both the verbal and nonverbal conversation.

Earlier it was noted that people with an individualistic orientation are likely to confront problems directly and loudly, clearly state their feelings, and sometimes speak at great length. Winning the point may be very important to these individuals. Conversely, those with a collectivistic orientation are likely to express their thoughts indirectly, want to avoid confrontation or have mediated problem resolution, and are more interested in getting along than in making a point. Their personal needs are subordinate to the common good. The development office manager may need to mediate these differences and help those with an individualistic schema slow down, be mindful of letting others save face, and think about the long-term good of the group. In contrast, those with a collectivistic orientation may need to be reminded to speak about their feelings, discuss problems, and distance the problem from the individual (Ting-Toomey and others, 2000). It is appropriate for the manager to set standards of behavior in conflict with an individual's culture as long as clear and specific justifications are presented as to why the individual must fit the desired norm (Kandola and Fullerton, 1994).

Facilitate dialogue to establish difference. Once individuals understand what they have in common, the stage is set for meaningful communication exploring differences. At this point exploring the different schema people hold can enhance understanding. An appropriate goal is to help staff move from an ethnocentric to an ethnorelative orientation (Hecht and others, forthcoming). Development office leadership can, for instance, invite staff to share how their cultures use different approaches to deciding what is appropriate behavior. The conversation might explore staff members' different perspectives based on Hofstede's four dimensions of culture (1996): (1) individualism versus collectivism, (2) large or small power distance, (3) strong or weak uncertainty avoidance, and

(4) masculinity versus femininity. In the process, help the staff recognize that people are motivated differently. For instance, individualists are more likely to be motivated by personal achievement. They need to know that achieving "diversity competence" can help them understand others, achieve their communication goals, and raise more money. In contrast, those from a collectivistic orientation are likely to be motivated by what is best for the long-term good of the organization and the work group. Thus they will understand the importance of "diversity competence" if it is presented as helping people get along better, avoiding embarrassment, and bringing people closer together.

Alternatively, some development offices have found it helpful to engage the staff in personality profiles like the Myers-Briggs Type Indicator (Hirsch and Kummerow, 1990). After the staff has taken the assessment and if they are willing to share the results, fruitful conversations can occur about how individuals gather information (sensing or intuition), how they make decisions (thinking or feeling), and how they are energized (extroverted or introverted). This sharing of information reveals the schema people hold, thus facilitating understanding.

If the staff is willing, invite them to share cultural experiences around significant holidays and life events such as weddings and funerals. Rituals are an important way of demonstrating what is important to a culture (Werner and Baxter, 1994). In the process be sure to welcome difference and reinforce the need for understanding different schema. By understanding others' schema, people are likely to feel more confident they can judge how others are likely to react during the communication setting. They will approach communication with diverse others with less anxiety and uncertainty.

Help people communicate mindfully by clarifying and addressing barriers. As noted earlier, communication is ubiquitous because people are always doing it, often without thinking. To have meaningful communication, however, people need to communicate mindfully. Mindful communication involves consciously thinking about what others are trying to say, being attentive to their schema, and constructing thoughtful responses that meet the needs of the speaker and the listener.

To help the development office staff communicate mindfully, consider asking individuals to identify what makes them uncomfortable. Address those issues in further conversation. For instance, the development office may have some collectivist employees who believe it is very important to get along and who are unlikely to directly face conflict. When confronted directly by a coworker from an individualistic perspective, the collectivist employee might be offended. Development office leadership can help these employees recognize they can adopt a more appropriate communication style that matches the style of the other. Without mindful conversation individuals from diverse backgrounds may have similar commitment to the organization's mission but miss their shared interests because of miscommunication and lack of trust (Schneider and Northcraft, 1999).

In essence, development office leadership is helping people develop competence in intercultural communication. Dimensions of interpersonal communication competence include capabilities such as the ability to self-disclose personal information, develop empathy, be relaxed in the social setting, be assertive without denying others their rights, effectively manage the interaction, achieve goals, and satisfy needs (Rubin and Martin, 1994). Other researchers have identified as important such things as "[taking] into consideration other people's perspectives, feelings, or thoughts," knowing another culture's "history, traditions, values, and customs," and adapting to the other person's culture (Redmond, 2000, p. 153). Development office leadership can help employees move toward the ethnorelative stage of seeking cultural difference (Hammer and Bennett, 2001). Leadership should work toward the goal of helping staff recognize other cultural perspectives and, where appropriate, integrate them into the workplace repertoire.

Unify the staff through commitment to the mission and organizational values. Once the staff has developed an affinity for each other and learned to appreciate differences, it is important to seek everyone's recommitment to the common goal: meeting the organization's mission. Development office leadership can remind the staff why the organization's mission is so important and in the process unify the staff so they focus on meeting the mission. This effort provides "in-group socialization" so all are working together. Leadership needs to help the staff recognize that they should be unified in their goal of achieving the organization's mission but that the mission is achieved by using individual differences.

Step 3: Monitor success

As with any important endeavor, progress should be monitored and positive experiences reinforced. Establishing a culture that encourages and accepts difference, being mindful of resistance and resolving conflicts, and providing continuing experiences are important components of maintaining a development office that embraces diversity.

Establish a culture that encourages and accepts difference. Some cohesion is necessary for the efficient functioning of the overall organization, but embracing differences and the wealth of experience they reflect also is important. Consider how the organization is communicating with its employees and the messages that are being presented, not just in the issuance of policy and memos but in the many other forms of communication. Pacanowsky and O'Donnell-Trujillo (1983) suggest that organizational communication be considered as cultural performances—that is, interactive, episodic, and improvisational communications that have contextual meanings. Development office leadership may find it helpful to examine the messages the organization is providing about diversity in the following "performances":

• *Rituals.* Each organization, individual, and group within the organization performs rituals on a regular basis, rituals that give consistency, structure, and comfort to the participants. Examine the rituals to see if they are consistent with the diversity message. For instance, one nonprofit organization recognized that the annual party invited employees' husbands or wives, shunning gay and lesbian employees who were in relationships but were not allowed to marry. The office changed the wording on invitations to include significant others, thus achieving congruence with the organization's message of being inclusive.

- *Passion.* Many development offices have corporate stories that are told about their founding or significant events. Colleagues may tell personal stories, perhaps about soliciting gifts or successes attained. Development office leadership may wish to examine the banter and stories shared in the office to see if they are communicating a message consistent with the diversity efforts.

- *Sociability.* Much of the conversation in the office is informal, such as the courtesies or pleasantries that are exchanged during the workday, at the coffee pot or in the parking lot. These encounters can provide an opportunity for individuals to share information that will build a sense of affinity and gain understanding of difference. Development office leadership should question if these conversations are inclusive of all employees or if there is a difference in the way people are reacting to each other in informal conversations.

- *Politics.* Development office leadership should examine how power, influence, and control are represented in the office. Appropriate questions to ask include the following: Are demonstrations of power sensitive to those who have different perspectives on Hofstede's power distance (1996)? Are allies or work groups diverse? Does leadership welcome input from diverse groups of employees?

- *Enculturation.* People learn the office culture and figure out what is expected and what type of behavior is appropriate. Development office leadership may wish to examine training and mentoring programs (both the formal presentations and the informal hallway conversations) to ensure the messages delivered are consistent with the organization's intended diversity communication.

Be mindful of those who will resist and resolve conflicts. Individuals are most comfortable communicating in homogeneous groups. By asking people to embrace diversity, the development office manager is requesting that they work outside their normal comfort area. Therefore be aware that small groups of employees may gather and "without malicious intention, develop their own independent social networks" (Schneider and Northcraft, 1999, p. 1452). These small groups can negate the benefits of bringing together diverse individuals, and they may even lose interest in communicating with diverse others. Development office leadership may have to have individual conversations with those who resist or give these individuals additional experiences so they move along the continuum from ethnocentric to ethnorelative.

Because diverse people bring different schema to the workplace, conflicts and misunderstandings will naturally develop. Analyze the source of the misunderstandings and help the parties resolve the issues. Recognize that communication style may exacerbate the problem. Individualists may need to be encouraged to say less, be less assertive, and "pay attention to group members" (Triandis, Brislin, and Hui, 1988, p. 282). Conversely, collectivists may need to be encouraged to say more, be emotionally detached from the events, and not feel threatened by competition (Triandis, Brislin, and Hui, 1988; Gudykunst, 1998). Development office leadership may need to moderate and facilitate these conversations.

When observing someone else's behavior, many individuals will attribute the cause of the behavior to internal characteristics such as the person's personality or to external factors such as the situation (Heider, 1958; Fiske and Taylor, 1991). People from collectivistic cultures will focus on attributes indicative of the other person's background and social status, whereas those from individualistic cultures will attribute actions to the other person's attitudes, values, and beliefs. In both cases, people will tend to blame the person more than the situation. Development office leadership can depersonalize the conflict and help build understanding by shifting the focus away from blaming others to looking at the situational factors that influenced the actions.

Provide continuing experiences and monitor success. The development office staff grow and change as they are provided additional experiences and exposure to diversity issues. Their reactions to diversity will become more sophisticated and complex as they have more experiences (Hammer and Bennett, 2001). Through continued exposure, employees should move through the ethnocentric stages of denial, defense, and minimization to the ethnorelative stages of acceptance, adaptation, and integration.

As leadership monitors the success of the efforts to incorporate diversity into the development office, it may be useful to remember that the workplace culture will change. This change can parallel the three stages of growth identified in *Building a High Performing Diverse Chapter* (Association of Fundraising Professionals, 1995), which suggests organizations move through a three-stage continuum as they learn to embrace diversity. In the first stage, *exclusive*, organizations exhibit "conflict, stagnation . . . no outside influences, and crisis management," and they are "steeped in rules and hierarchy" (p. 4). In the second stage, *passive*, organizations embrace "status quo, sporadic, scattered efforts, [and] tentative, unrewarding plan[s]," not showing "much initiative or response, except to pressure" (p. 4). In the final, enlightened stage, *inclusive*, organizations are identified as being "dynamic, innovative, visionary, collaborative, responsive" (p. 4). Using these guidelines can be a good way to measure success in the development office. Is the organization basically passive about incorporating diversity and welcoming difference? Does the office show signs of being at the exclusive stage, or is the organization already dynamic, innovative, and visionary—qualities associated with being inclusive? Occasionally reviewing these guidelines may be helpful to the development office leadership.

Conclusion

This chapter has recommended that a communication perspective be used to manage diversity in the development office. This perspective suggests that diversity be recognized as an element of identity and focuses on communicating by understanding the schema people create. The recommendations made in this chapter can help development office leaders promote an organizational culture that welcomes and embraces diversity.

References

Adler, N. "Communicating Across Cultural Barriers." In J. Billsberry (ed.), *The Effective Manager: Perspectives and Illustrations.* Thousand Oaks, Calif.: Sage, 1996.

Armstrong, G. B., and Kaplowitz, S. A. "Sociolinguistic Inference and Intercultural Coorientation: A Bayesian Model of Communicative Competence in Intercultural Interaction." *Human Communication Research,* 2001, *27*(3), 350–381.

Association of Fundraising Professionals. *Building a High Performing Diverse Chapter.* Washington, D.C.: Association of Fundraising Professionals, 1995.

Axtell, R. E. *Gestures: The Do's and Taboos of Body Language Around the World.* New York: Wiley, 1998.

Bell, R. A., and Daly, J. A. "The Affinity-Seeking Function of Communication." *Communication Monographs,* 1984, *51*(2), 91–115.

Berger, C. R., and Calabrese, R. "Some Explorations in Initial Interactions and Beyond." *Human Communication Research,* 1975, *1*(2), 99–112.

Cronen, V. E., Pearce, W. B., and Harris, L. M. "The Coordinated Management of Meaning: A Theory of Communication." In F.E.X. Dance (ed.), *Human Communication Theory: Comparative Essays.* New York: Harper-Collins, 1982.

Feghali, E. K. "Arab Cultural Communication Patterns." *International Journal of Intercultural Relations,* 1997, *21*(3), 345–378.

Fischer, M. "Respecting the Individual, Valuing Diversity: Equity in Philanthropy and Fund Raising." In D. F. Burlingame (ed.), *Critical Issues in Fund Raising.* New York: Wiley, 1997.

Fiske, S. T., and Taylor, S. E. *Social Cognition.* (2nd ed.) New York: McGraw-Hill, 1991.

Gao, G. "'Don't Take My Word for It'—Understanding Chinese Speaking Practices." *International Journal of Intercultural Relations,* 1998, *22*(2), 163–186.

Gudykunst, W. B. "Cross-Cultural Comparisons." In C. R. Berger and S. H. Chaffee (eds.), *Handbook of Communication Science.* Thousand Oaks, Calif.: Sage, 1987.

Gudykunst, W. B. "Applying Anxiety/Uncertainty Management (AUM) Theory to Intercultural Adjustment Training." *International Journal of Intercultural Relations,* 1998, *22*(2), 227–250.

Gudykunst, W. B., Matsumoto, Y., Ting-Toomey, S., and Nishida, T. "The Influence of Cultural Individualism-Collectivism, Self Construals, and Individual Values on Communication Styles Across Cultures." *Human Communication Research,* 1996, *22*(4), 510–543.

Gudykunst, W. B., and Nishida, T. "Individual and Cultural Influences on Uncertainty Reduction." *Communication Monographs,* 1984, *51*(1), 23–36.

Gudykunst, W. B., and Nishida, T. "Anxiety, Uncertainty, and Perceived Effectiveness of Communication Across Relationships and Cultures." *International Journal of Intercultural Relations,* 2001, *25*(1), 55–71.

Gudykunst, W. B., and Ting-Toomey, S. "Ethnic Identity, Language and Communication Breakdowns." In H. Giles and W. P. Robinson (eds.), *Handbook of Language and Social Psychology.* New York: Wiley, 1990.

Hammer, M. R., and Bennett, M. J. "Measuring Intercultural Competence: The Intercultural Development Inventory." Paper presented at the International Communication Association Meeting, Washington, D.C., May 2001.

Hecht, M. L., and Faulkner, S. L. "Sometimes Jewish, Sometimes Not: The Closeting of Jewish American Identity." *Communication Studies*, 2000, *51*(4), 372–387.

Hecht, M. L., and others. "Looking Through Northern Exposure at Jewish American Identity and the Communication Theory of Identity." *Journal of Communication*, forthcoming.

Heider, F. *The Psychology of Interpersonal Relations*. New York: Wiley, 1958.

Hirsch, S. K., and Kummerow, J. M. *Introduction to Type in Organizations*. Palo Alto, Calif.: Consulting Psychologists Press, 1990.

Hofstede, G. *Cultures and Organizations: Software of the Mind*. New York: McGraw-Hill, 1991.

Hofstede, G. "The Cultural Relativity of Organizational Practices and Theories." In J. Billsberry (ed.), *The Effective Manager: Perspectives and Illustrations*. Thousand Oaks, Calif.: Sage, 1996.

Hraba, J., and Hoiberg, E. "Identical Origins of Modern Theories of Ethnicity." *Sociological Quarterly*, 1983, *24*(3), 381–391.

Kandola, R., and Fullerton, J. *Managing the Mosaic: Diversity in Action*. London: Institute of Personnel and Development, 1994.

Kandola, R., and Fullerton, J. "Diversity: More Than Just an Empty Slogan." In J. Billsberry (ed.), *The Effective Manager: Perspectives and Illustrations*. Thousand Oaks, Calif.: Sage, 1996.

Kim, M.-S., Shin, H.-C., and Cai, D. "Cultural Influences on the Preferred Forms of Requesting and Re-Requesting." *Communication Monographs*, 1998, *65*(1), 47–66.

Lawthom, R. "Against All Odds: Managing Diversity." In N. Chmiel (ed.), *Introduction to Work and Organizational Psychology*. Cambridge, Mass.: Blackwell, 2000.

Li, H. Z. "Communicating Information in Conversations: A Cross-Cultural Comparison." *International Journal of Intercultural Relations*, 1999, *23*(3), 387–409.

Martin, M. M., and Rubin, R. B. "Affinity-Seeking in Initial Interactions." *Southern Communication Journal*, 1998, *63*(2), 131–143.

McGrath, J. E., Berdahl, J. L., and Arrow, H. "No One Has It All But Groups Do: Diversity as a Collective, Complex, Dynamic Property of Groups." In S. Jackson and M. Ruderman (eds.), *Diversity in Work Teams*. Washington, D.C.: American Psychological Association Press, 1995.

Pacanowsky, M. E., and O'Donnell-Trujillo, N. "Organizational Communication as Cultural Performance." *Communication Monographs*, 1983, *50*(2), 126–147.

Park, B., and Judd, C. M. "Measures and Models of Perceived Group Variability." *Journal of Personality and Social Psychology*, 1990, *59*(2), 173–191.

Redmond, M. V. "Cultural Distance as a Mediating Factor Between Stress and Intercultural Communication Competence." *International Journal of Intercultural Relations*, 2000, *24*(1), 151–159.

Rubin, R. B., and Martin, M. M. "Development of a Measure of Interpersonal Communication Competence." *Communication Research Reports*, 1994, *11*(1), 33–44.

Rubin, R. B., Rubin, A. M., and Martin, M. M. "The Role of Self-Disclosure and Self-Awareness in Affinity-Seeking Competence." *Communication Research Reports*, 1993, *10*(2), 115–127.

Schneider, S. K., and Northcraft, G. B. "Three Social Dilemmas of Workforce Diversity in Organizations: A Social Identity Perspective." *Human Relations*, 1999, *52*(11), 1445–1467.

Shallenberger, D. "Professional and Openly Gay: A Narrative Study of the Experience." In J. Billsberry (ed.), *The Effective Manager: Perspectives and Illustrations*. Thousand Oaks, Calif.: Sage, 1996.

Steele, C. M., and Aronson, J. "Stereotype Threat and the Intellectual Test Performance of African Americans." *Journal of Personality and Social Psychology*, 1995, *69*(5), 797–811.

Ting-Toomey, S., and others. "Ethnic/Cultural Identity Salience and Conflict Styles in Four U.S. Ethnic Groups." *International Journal of Intercultural Relations*, 2000, *24*(2), 47–81.

Triandis, H. C., Brislin, R., and Hui, C. H. "Cross-Cultural Training Across the Individualism-Collectivism Divide." *International Journal of Intercultural Relations*, 1988, *12*(3), 269–289.

Werner, C. M., and Baxter, L. A. "Temporal Qualities of Relationships: Organismic, Transactional, and Dialectical Views." In M. L. Knapp and G. R. Miller (eds.), *Handbook of Interpersonal Communication*. Thousand Oaks, Calif.: Sage, 1994.

WILLIAM F. BARTOLINI *is director of constituent development programs for Kent State University in Kent, Ohio. He serves on the national board of directors of the Association of Fundraising Professionals and chairs its Diversity Committee.*

Organizational development and fundraising professionals, as well as board volunteers, have the opportunity to cross boundaries that divide people in other sectors. Whether we view this opportunity with apprehension or enthusiasm depends on our heritage, experiences, beliefs, and vision. Historically, nonprofit boards have offered limited opportunities to develop diverse leadership.

4

Beyond representation: Building diverse board leadership teams

Maria Gitin

OVER THE YEARS, dialogue on board diversification has evolved from focus on the importance of representing constituents, to "doing the right thing," which is characterized by opponents as "political correctness," to the current widely held view that a nondiverse board is missing key potential donors and opinion leaders. Diverse leaders can expand knowledge, create new resources, and open doors to partnerships necessary to fulfill an organization's mission.

Recommended strategies for board diversification must be understood in the context of the deeply divided society of the United States. Although North American cultural issues are the result of a unique history, most elements of diversity planning will apply in other countries as well. By the year 2015 the nonwhite portion of the U.S. population is expected to increase to 30 percent

NEW DIRECTIONS FOR PHILANTHROPIC FUNDRAISING, NO. 34, WINTER 2001 © WILEY PERIODICALS, INC.

(Changing Our World, 2001). In many communities, including large areas of California, the nonwhite population is already at 50 percent (Changing Our World, 2000).

Despite heroic efforts on the part of diverse public and nonprofit sector leaders and their allies, gaps between rich and poor, and between people of color and whites, have increased over the past decade:

- Poverty rates for full-time U.S. workers have stayed constant in the past two decades while wealth concentration in the uppermost tiers of income has increased (Changing Our World, 2001).

- Although Hispanic males have the highest labor force participation of any ethnic group, according to a March 9, 2000, report by the National Council on La Raza, the number of low-income Hispanic households has doubled in the past twenty years (Pementel, 2002).

- The African American unemployment rate was reported at 9 percent, compared with 5.6 percent for the overall population, in January 2002 (Hunt, 2002).

- The financial wealth of the top 1 percent of households now exceeds the combined wealth of the bottom 95 percent (Wolff, 1998).

- As of 1997, the net worth of white families was eight times that of African Americans and twelve times that of Hispanics (Wolff, 1998).

- A study of intergroup relations conducted by Princeton Survey Research Associates (2000, p. ix) reports that "[o]nly 29% of respondents are satisfied with how well different groups in society get along with each other and that 75% feel that racial, religious and ethnic tension is a very serious or somewhat serious problem."

- The National Asian Pacific American League ([2002]) documented more than 250 hate crime incidents toward Asians since September 11, 2001, the date of attacks on New York and Washington, D.C., buildings that left 2,800 people dead. In all cases where there were witnesses, the perpetrators mistook the victims for Arabs.

Despite the discouraging data, many nonprofit thinkers believe that our sector must take the lead in pluralism. Public tax-exempt status, nonprofit missions and their fulfillment and the success of programs depend in great part on the success of inclusion. Diversification is key to keeping the social sector relevant and sustainable. The social sector is also a potentially potent counterforce to the prevailing corporate and military domination of public and political thought. In the social sector creative responses to poverty, violence, racism, and other injustices can be generated with mission foremost. Innovations in art, education, environmental protection, and health care can be developed with marketing and funding concerns in their appropriate supporting role.

Board diversity defined

Philanthropy means "love of humanity" or, as defined by the *New American Heritage Dictionary*, "the love of mankind and the effort to increase the well-being of mankind." As defined by Robert Payton (1988), former director of the Center on Philanthropy at Indiana University, philanthropy is "voluntary action for the public good."

Creating an environment that attracts philanthropy, developing skills that generate philanthropy, and building an infrastructure to sustain philanthropic activity are primary tasks of board and staff leadership teams. Contributions of time, talent, and treasure are commonly accepted manifestations of philanthropy, with nonprofit board leadership calling for all three. If philanthropy expresses love of humanity, then how broadly or narrowly that humanity is defined opens or closes the doors of diversity. Organizational development and fundraising professionals, as well as board volunteers, have the opportunity to cross over many of the boundaries that divide people in other sectors. Whether we view this opportunity with apprehension or enthusiasm depends on our heritage, past experience, beliefs, and vision. Historically, boards of nonprofit institutions have offered limited opportunities for development of diverse leadership.

As I and Charles R. Stephens (1999, p. 18) wrote in *Advancing Philanthropy*, "Scholars and leaders in the Third Sector tend to think of diversity as a disease requiring a cure by Philanthropy. That belief is reflected in the ongoing delimiting language and activities of The Third Sector. While the profession is diversifying, and board leadership is beginning to diversify, little change can be expected as long as the mindset of those who study, think, and write about this phenomenon remains rooted in European-American, Anglo-Saxon, Protestant values."

The Association of Fundraising Professionals Diversity Committee defines diversity as "1. The quality or state of being different. 2. The quality or state of encompassing people of a different race, ethnicity, gender, religion, physical ability, age, sexual orientation and income as regards to the composition of staff and board" (AFP, 2001).

Developed by Maria Gitin & Associates with Charles R. Stephens, the national training models titled "Diversity in Fundraising Curriculum" and "Embracing Diversity: The Search for Common Ground" use the following definition of diversity: "differences which significantly affect the way we experience ourselves and are treated by others." Categories of diversity may include ethnicity, gender, sexual orientation, age, religion, class and economic status, being a parent or childless, and physical or mental ability or challenge. Additional private identities, such as recovering alcoholic, incest survivor, and other identities that affect us profoundly while not being obvious to others, may also be included (Maria Gitin & Associates, 1997).

Years ago we included "race" as a category. However, most diversity practitioners and ethnic leaders find the categories of Caucasian, Negroid, and Mongolian outmoded. "Ethnicity" is a more encompassing classification, defined as a social group with similar physical, cultural, or religious roots, including race. Ethnicity generates greater affiliation, as evidenced by ethnic warfare throughout the world and ethnic tensions in our own country. Positive expressions of identity are demonstrated through cultural arts, cuisine, mutual benefit societies, religious communities, political action committees, and cooperative economic partnerships within immigrant ethnic communities, to cite only a few examples. Yet most white Americans, even in the philanthropic sector and even while wanting to diversify, are unaware of what affects ethnic populations and what their contributions *to* nonprofit boards could be.

For board development projects, at Maria Gitin & Associates we primarily focus on ethnicity, with attention also paid to age, class, sexual orientation, and physical and mental challenges or abilities. For board diversification purposes clients most frequently state the groups. The majority of boards we work with report that most board members are within a ten- to twenty-year age range of each other. Environmental and social justice groups and independent schools often have younger board members, whereas arts and higher education tend to have the oldest board members. Social, human, and health care service boards tend to cluster around the age group of those who were young during the time their cause came into prominence and their agency was founded. In subsequent decades these boards seldom continue to recruit new young board members. As the organization matures, so do board members, who may also change careers and no longer stay active in their fields.

Most board members are in the same social and professional class, even when ethnic diversity is present. Similarities in age and income tend to mirror other homogeneous aspects of boards because most recruitment is accomplished through nondiverse social and professional networks.

The role of pluralism in redefining board leadership

Oft-stated reasons for board diversity include the need to reach diverse constituents and potential donors, accurate representation of constituents, reflection of organizational values, requirements of funders, and the need to broaden the knowledge base for policy decisions. Beyond these persuasive reasons, we know from worldwide demographic data that diversity is not an ideal but a fact. Consider the following facts, as presented in an article in *Advancing Philanthropy* (Gitin and Stephens, 1999, p. 20):

The majority of people in the world are not European or American, they are Asian. The most populous religion in the world is not Christianity, it is Islam. The majority of people in the world are women, not men, youth, not adults. The economic dominance of primarily male, white-owned corporations continues to influence institutions and board development out of proportion to their numbers, and is likely to do so for some time.

More than 50% of the people on earth experience their lives and generate their values from the female perspective, yet male language such as "targets" and "campaigns" dominate our educational courses and fundraising literature. More than 80% of the people in the world do not have "white" skin, yet most U.S. and many international institutions are organized and led solely by people of European-American descent. 10% of all people are gay and lesbian; yet planned giving courses continue to offer only married couples and widow or widower as potential prospect examples. The economically dominant, not numerically represented culture, defines the values and beliefs, which drive the mission, message, and media through which we currently conduct the business of philanthropy, limiting our potential.

Success that begins with values

Consider the implications of the belief, which we encounter in the philanthropic sector, that a civil society and democratic institutions require shared values and that diversity is a threat to shared values. Bruce Sievers (1995) explores this topic in his thought-provoking article "Can Philanthropy Solve the Problems of Civil Society?" In his article Sievers discusses the limitations of outcome-based social programs, which value individual freedom and pluralism to the degree that there are no values communicated either in the delivery of services or on the part of the providers. Real change, in behavior, in caring for the environment, in appreciating art, and so forth, depends on internalized values. We cannot expect lasting change to be generated by even the best projects and programs unless the philanthropic sector finds a way to integrate civil society to be fully inclusive.

If a society, in the United States or in any country, is to be value based, the question becomes, Whose values? The U.S. Constitution ensures equal opportunity for all, but there are some people the government would rather not know exist, as is evident by the U.S. military's "Don't ask, don't tell" policy toward gays and lesbians. If a person cannot be his or her essential sexual self, how equal can opportunity be?

If we are going to create a "civil society," it is not likely to happen around the nonprofit boardroom table, given the current composition of most boards. Nor is it likely to occur by simply inviting people of diverse heritage, age, gender, and physical ability to serve on a board. Many people who have been locked out of nonprofit power structures of the past are no longer seeking entry and are generating entirely new access to power. Ethnic communities and other affinity groups have always networked at the local level through faith-based, social, and economic partnerships. Today national and international organizations and conferences such as Hispanics in Philanthropy and Blacks in Philanthropy have their own publications, listservs, and Web sites. The scarcity of diverse candidates may actually reflect a lack of candidates willing to serve on boards dominated by old nondiverse majorities. Diverse boards seem to have little difficulty attracting additional diversity.

At a recent board diversity seminar, a young Latino spoke of waiting fifteen years before being considered ready to serve on a community nonprofit board. A long-recognized leader in his own community, he found an attitude of elitism on the board after finally joining and was surprised that the board members did not recognize the barriers they created that limited his participation.

The traditional approach to board diversification

While recognizing the variety of diversities that enrich board composition, ethnic diversity is used as an example because of the predominance of interest in cultural pluralism. The customary approach to recruiting ethnic diversity has been de facto Eurocentric because the majority of boards are composed of white people. According to a study by the National Center for Nonprofit Boards (1999), minorities make up only 15 percent of board members while constituting 28 percent of the U.S. population.

In board recruitment current board members are asked to identify contacts they may have among people of color, women, or other diverse groups. In the past many nonprofits were satisfied to have "representative" board members who came from diverse backgrounds. These individuals may or may not have been representative of, or seen as leaders in, their own communities.

With the evolution of boards from management to governance bodies (Miller, Fletcher, and Abzug, 1999), recruitment focus has shifted to specific skill sets and leadership qualifications that will further an organization's mission. Board diversity plans seek to splice experience, education, and ability qualifiers with ethnicity and other demographics to get what is popularly known as a "twofer," meaning "two for one"—skills plus ethnicity. With the requirements leaning heavily toward skills derived from university education and professional experience, where racism still limits opportunities, the base of recruits of color thins out just as it does in the corporate boardrooms of America.

Challenges and limitations to board diversity approaches

A detailed description of the categories of representation—delegate, trustee, symbolic, and practical—is found in *Perspectives on Nonprofit Board Diversity* (Miller, Fletcher, and Abzug, 1999). In general, board diversity initiatives begin with the question, Who are we missing? rather than the question, How do we need to change to attract those we want to recruit?

The relationship-building skills that leaders use to attract philanthropic dollars seem to disappear during board recruitment. As I and Stephens (1999) point out, Fundraising is about relationships. Successful development professionals know how to listen effectively. They build bridges between the ideals and programs of the institutions they represent and the needs of donors and funders. They know how to seek, find and create the common ground that enables the gift exchange to take place. The issue of board diversity may be ignored during recruitment in order to avoid the painful knowledge of economic inequity between people of color and whites, as well as the desire to avoid dealing with bias that may surface in the institution. Assessment responses from diverse board members frequently identify specific ways a board can become more accessible to diverse constituents. However, in my work as a board development consultant, when I present strategies to increase diversity—for example, inviting nonboard community members to assist with the search for candidates of color—these recommendations are frequently rejected as "reverse racism" or "quotas."

We live in an increasingly multiethnic, and at the same time increasingly segregated, society, far from the "melting pot" dream of post–World War II Americans (National Center for Nonprofit Boards, 1999). Most white people (80 percent) live in neighborhoods where they are the majority with African Americans comprising less than 1 percent of the population (West, 1993). It is a well-known saying among preachers, credited to Martin Luther King Jr., that "Sunday morning is the most segregated hour in America." For many, the opportunity to form multicultural relationships is limited to the workplace, where discrimination limits opportunity for diverse teamwork as well.

Other barriers to diversification are the very human fear of change, the uncertainty, and the discomfort new people and new ideas are sure to generate. Renowned nonprofit leader John Gardner (1994, p. 4) once said, "The ancient human impulse to hate and fear the tribe in the next valley, the ethnic group on the next block, those who are not like us, is deep-seated."

Assumptions and concerns that impede diversity

Breaking through the self-limiting nature of board composition requires questioning assumptions and dealing with concerns. One limiting assumption is that the traditional management structure or even the governance model of boards is the most effective. In my experience, I have found that many boards are unfamiliar with the results of the recent studies and research on governance and their potential application in diverse environments. Recommended reading includes the National Center for Nonprofit Boards California board summit report (2000) and *Improving the Performance of Governing Boards* (Chait, Holland, and Taylor, 1999). Studying these and other reports on governance can set the stage for new thinking and planning, to which we can add and emphasize diversity.

Another assumption is that any one group considers itself nondiverse, that is, "normal." As Fischer (1995) says, "This is only possible for people with white skin because the world is so constructed that it reflects primarily the experience of those with wealth, with power and who, in much of the world, also have light skin. Even those with light skin who do not have power or wealth indirectly benefit from their skin color because they are less oppressed." Acceptance of this "white privilege" and recognition of our own differences are painful but essential steps to overcoming the denial that can alienate us from prospective board members.

A concern that may block action is the fear of actually focusing on race or ethnicity, or any other diversity, as a primary board goal. Diversity is still relegated to the status of a program or a problem to be solved rather than embraced as central to philanthropy. How often do we hear the lament "We want diversity on our board, but we can't find qualified Latinos (or people with disabilities, or youth, and so on) willing to serve"? There are often complaints that "they" (whichever group is not in the majority) "stick to themselves."

People of color may justly complain, "They just don't get it," when speaking of European American efforts to cross cultural and racial boundaries. People of all kinds of diversities, including gays, lesbians, bisexuals, and people with disabilities, look to social sector boards to see if they and their issues are well represented. We need to open the doors to diverse interests and see this as key to serving the common good and fulfilling mission and purpose.

An environment that welcomes diversity

An important element of diversification is the willingness to accept differences. We are not all alike, and the goal is not to become alike but to create cross-cultural dialogue and effective leadership teams. We are all diverse. Even individuals who label themselves "plain vanilla" or "fifty-seven flavors" are a unique blend of ethnicity, faith, cultural heritage, and class origins. Personal identifiers (such as sexual orientation, physical and mental ability, or age) and private identities (such as adopted, divorced, recovering alcoholic, or survivor of abuse) all add to our diversity (Maria Gitin & Associates, 1997). Diversity training and group processes that allow individuals to see themselves and each other as unique and valuable contributors to the board can be useful in countering stereotypes and in discovering common values.

Vision and values that attract diversity

The importance of achieving diversity is seldom seen stated with the strength of commitment evident in the national YWCA mission statement (YWCA of the U.S.A., 2002):

Our mission is to empower women and girls and to eliminate racism. . . . Strengthened by diversity, the Association draws together members who strive to create opportunities for women's growth, leadership and power in order to attain a common vision: peace, justice, freedom and dignity for all people.

The Association will thrust its collective power toward the elimination of racism wherever it exists and by any means necessary.

Organizations that hold diversity as a core value will do "whatever it takes" to achieve diversity. Diversity requires a long-term commitment and a significant investment of time, money, and resources. Diversity must be included in mission statements, board recruitment materials, and staff-hiring announcements. Ongoing cultural competence assessment, training, and evaluation are essential to creating change. Diversity values must not only be claimed and proclaimed; they must be practiced in every aspect of the organization, from planning events to designing donor acknowledgment levels. Inclusiveness in language, visual displays, physical accessibility, and scheduling to honor and avoid conflict with diverse heritage celebrations demonstrates a commitment to diversity.

For the majority culture, clinging to outdated and ineffective slogans such as "We are color-blind," "Don't ask, don't tell," or "We are all one" stands in the way of accepting the reality of others and developing successful strategies for board diversity. Minority culture members may need a lot of convincing that there is value to serving on a board. These and other challenges can be overcome through planning, training, action, and commitment to diversity.

People from the historical minority may tire of the dominant culture habits of boards that can be affected by divergent views of time, money, power, and even meeting facilitation. Predominantly white boards must demonstrate commitment by beginning with self-education and then creating relationships by being useful to the communities they want to access. Individual or group action can build relationships that allow us to escape the tautology of white-led diversity efforts.

Being an ally, taking a behind-the-scenes role in support of a diverse community, is an effective bridge builder. During the civil rights movement, one of the valuable experiences for many of the white student workers was participating in well-organized, effective African American–led civil rights organizations. These organizations were capable of integrating to accept white support and mostly patient with our education. For many students from the north and west, this was the first opportunity we had to work in teams led by student and adult African Americans.

I know of a Jewish woman who volunteered behind the scenes for years with a local NAACP chapter, helping plan and raise funds for a community Kwanza celebration. The most important things she did were to not ask for or even accept recognition, to work during the celebration, stirring pots in the kitchen so the African American leaders could be out front with the crowd, and to get out of the way once the event became established. In addition to forming some close friendships, now when she asks for access and information from the African American community, they are readily given.

Nationally known diversity trainer and speaker Alvin B. Herring, CEO and founder of Side by Side: Building Communities of Hope, in an oral presentation to the Association of Fundraising Professionals Conference in San Diego in 2001, talks about "bridge people": those who are able to reach across differences and connect in a meaningful and useful way with others, working toward a common goal. Successful board development requires that all leaders become bridge people.

Time, patience, willingness to explain, listen, and ask, a solid plan with clear benchmarks, and a commitment to ongoing training can create an environment that truly welcomes diversity.

Questions to consider

In their efforts to increase board diversity, nonprofit organizations will find it useful to ask themselves the following questions.

1. Can European American leaders reevaluate the belief that their culture and values are superior to others, particularly as defined by the male, white, Christian experience? Can those from the dominant culture affirm the experience, history, and contributions of others as completely valid?

2. Are we willing to recognize and examine assumptions about our own and others' groups and listen to these groups tell us how assumptions affect their willingness to participate?

Commitment to pluralism is evidenced by relentless self-assessment, evaluation, and input from diverse people, as well as by results. Outcome evaluation prevalent in programs must be institutionalized as a board practice.

3. Are we willing to take risks and ask questions in respectful ways that lead to greater understanding? Can those of us who care

about diversity, particularly white people, find a way to communicate more effectively and nondefensively?

Instead of intelligent discourse, we often succumb to simplistic sound bites. When we hear racist remarks in professional settings, see how facilities impose barriers to people with disabilities, or see that lack of an advanced degree stymies professional advancement, we may cringe but fail to respond by tackling the problems. Real dialogue and change require time, but we are impatient and weary. We give up and say, "We tried that, and it didn't work."

4. As we develop diverse recruitment teams, will we make the time to get to know one another instead of paving over one another's feelings with good intentions and stereotypes? Are we willing to be uncomfortable?

White skin and heterosexuality carry many advantages that are invisible to those who have them and that are blatantly offensive to those who do not. One of the most obvious advantages of being straight and white is that no matter how liberal we are, most of us can set aside our convictions for the length of a corporate fundraising campaign or a board meeting and simply fit in. The media, universities, the legal profession, and law enforcement are dominated by straight, white, middle- and upper-middle-class people, and their reflection is seen everywhere.

5. Can we learn to recognize and effectively confront racism, sexism, homophobia, ageism, classism, and ableism (prejudice against people with disabilities)?

Most nonprofits value cooperation and teamwork. Questioning plans, programs, and policies in light of their impact on diversity takes courage and effective communication skills.

The role of staff in board recruitment

Board governance or nominating committees should look to staff for recommendations and assistance with recruitment and cultivation. In many organizations the staff is more diverse than the board and has the opportunity to lead collaborative efforts that broaden diversity. When strategic restructuring between organizations takes place, board diversity may result as part of the merger or be increased to effectively serve the newly diverse organization.

Recruitment for diversity

Prior to recruitment the board should undertake rigorous self-assessment and cultural competence training. Cultural competence training teaches the practical application of diversity concepts. Training establishes commitment to the recruitment process and lays the groundwork for successful recruitment planning.

Prospecting and cultivating diverse board members

Encourage board members to attend and support cross-cultural community activities and to identify themselves as board members. Attend meetings and events that involve and attract diverse leaders. For example, the Japanese American Citizens League, Filipino America groups, NAACP, League of United Latin American Citizens, and Chinese, Arab, Latino, and Native American organizations often have guest speakers and events open to the entire community. Most diverse affinity groups have cultural and educational activities such as disability fairs or gay, lesbian, and bisexual events. These established organizations or new ones may attract the diversities the board wants represented. A staff member or board representative could speak to one of these organizations and inform it of a board opening. Provide written as well as oral information so that it can be passed on to potential candidates.

Applying the principles of diversity recruitment

Because it is natural to feel comfortable with people similar to ourselves, try to involve a representative of the constituency you are recruiting in the recruitment process. The best recruiter is the person most familiar with this group through their work, neighborhood, or personal relationships. This may mean being flexible with protocol so that a diverse staff member can take the lead for the whole recruitment process.

Do not recruit board members based solely on skin color, age, economic status, or any of the diversities the board desires to recruit. Identify one or more of the skill areas needed by the board and explore the potential candidate's interests.

Be straightforward. Let the potential candidate know that the board is trying to recruit people with disabilities or Latinos, people who were raised poor, seniors, gay men, lesbians, or whoever is missing from its composition.

In the cultivation phase find out everything prospective board members are interested in, not just what the recruitment team thinks they should undertake. If recruits are the first and only representatives of their groups, ask them early and often what barriers they observe, what could make their experience more enjoyable, and in what ways other board members could make them feel more welcome.

Be respectful and patient, and listen to feedback. Modify your approach based on the responses you receive.

Retention and renewal of diverse boards

Board member satisfaction should be assessed on a continuous basis. Commonly used board self-assessment tools are available from Board Source (formerly the National Center for Nonprofit Boards), the Association of Fundraising Professionals Resource Center, and other nonprofit training organizations. Inclusion of diversity in self-assessment is an important step toward staying current with board cultural competence.

Training

Even the most experienced board members benefit from annual board orientation and training, which offer opportunities to bond in a more relaxed environment than a board meeting. Plan orientation activities to include social, networking time, sharing of a meal or snack, and team-building exercises structured to foster cross-group communication. Training for boards might include cultural competence training, board staff roles and relations, board diversity planning, leadership training, and collaboration. Useful tools for board retreats and planning sessions include the Peter F. Drucker self-assessment strategic planning tool *The Courage to Lead* (Stern, 2001) and much of the National Center for Nonprofit Boards governance series. These tools can be adapted to emphasize and embed cultural competence and diversity goals. Most regional and community foundations and many other training organizations offer affordable courses on diversity and cultural competence. Budgeting for board orientation and training keeps a board up to date and demonstrates the value the organization places on board service.

Mentorship and coaching

Although training is invaluable, many organizations have difficulty carving out time and financial resources for extensive training. Some successful boards use buddy or mentor programs to bring newly elected members up to speed quickly. Mentoring can save time at board meetings, make members feel valued, and resolve issues that might lead to resignation. Usually, a more experienced member is assigned to a newer one, often among those who are serving on the same committee or task force. Make sure that no new members are assigned tasks or decision-making responsibility without all the tools and information they need to do a good job and make good decisions.

Board and committee chairs should seek opportunities to meet with individual board members, whether or not there appear to be problems. Board chairs should seek individual views on the success of the diversity initiative in the context of the work of the board.

Succession planning

Achieving initial diversity goals is not a signal to stop concentrating on the effort. A board that relies on a few people to support the diversity effort may find that motivation and impetus for implementation are lost when these supporters rotate off of the board, and it may be difficult to begin anew. Following one of the key principles of self-assessment is the Peter F. Drucker tool (Stern, 2001), "embed diversity" in every aspect of board development. Enroll your departing board members in recruiting their replacements. Board governance should be a standing committee, responsible for board development as a whole, not the old "seasonal work" nominating committee that only meets when a board vacancy is about to occur.

Diversity initiative strategies

Although there is no one-size-fits-all approach to diversity planning, as goals will differ among organizations, regions of the country, and parts of the world, there are some elements of diversity initiatives that seem to work well in any setting.

Institutionalize diversity

An institutional diversity action plan will be most effective if it is launched from within a powerful committee of the board, such as the governance committee, rather than relegated to a separate group. However, if the current board is nondiverse, planning may need to begin with a diversity team formed with staff and community members who are experienced and trained in setting and achieving diversity objectives. This group can advise the board in finding appropriate training and in developing the first diversity action plan.

To achieve success the diversity team or governance committee must have diverse leadership and membership. Goals must be articulated and incorporated into every program, not relegated to "minority" staff and board members. Internal and external training must be provided on an ongoing basis. Evaluation tools must be developed and used to assess progress and set new goals.

The Appendix at the end of this chapter shows a model board diversity plan for an organization with a mandate to recruit Latino board members. That model can be combined with, and adapted for, recruitment of any type of board members.

Ensure success through values

The ultimate success or failure of board diversity initiatives depends on some factors that seem beyond control, yet the social sector has great responsibility and ability to influence the political and economic environment, in our own countries and globally. I frequently notice that board members who have been active politically are more comfortable with differences of opinion and background than those who have not. It is essential to practice both honesty and inclusion in order to achieve the consensus and common ground that lead to shared values.

If we truly believe that democracy and inclusive institutions require shared values, then we must delve into the differences that inform these values and create together a new understanding of common ground. Change depends on internalizing values. Although individuals can make great strides, we cannot expect lasting change to be generated by even the best board leaders without the support of the entire social sector.

Success ensured through values

When a majority of nonprofit organizational leaders declare a commitment to diversity, results will follow. Success with pluralism in board leadership will expand our vision and potential to fulfill organizational goals, serve constituents, and manifest missions. Achieving true diversity will position organizations to become coalitions and peace builders in their communities and in the world. I can think of no endeavor more important.

Appendix: Model board diversity plan for Ideal Organization

Background and critical issues

This plan is based on a board assessment, results of a board diversity and cultural competence workshop, and a work plan developed by a board development team, augmented with recommendations from consultants. Ideal Organization staff is engaged in a cultural competence assessment that is focused on service delivery and workplace issues. Staff plans are shared with the board so that collaborative training and materials may be developed as appropriate. Following is an excerpt from the Ideal Organization board development plan:

The challenge

The board wants to stay representative yet become stronger and more effective through increased diversity, recruitment, and leadership training. The traditional representational board composition and role are being revisited with the goal of developing a more active and strategic governing body.

The strategy

The board development project purpose is to plan and strengthen these areas: structure, including potential role of advisory boards; board composition, including size and diversity; board and staff roles and relations; board election policies and procedures. During the process, board materials will be redesigned and board training offered to ensure cultural competence and an environment that welcomes diversity. A diverse consulting team facilitates this process.

Diversity assessment of current board

There is no question as to the value of diversity in this organization. Staff and board have historically been committed to multiculturalism. Ideal Organization has always had diverse board members and a strong affirmative action policy. However, there has been difficulty retaining a diverse board. According to their self-assessment, 95 percent of board members do not believe the current board has adequate diversity.

A major goal of the board development project is to achieve an appropriately diverse board. Although all types of diversity are important to this agency, priority recruitment will focus on improving ethnic and age balance. More than 80 percent of Ideal Organization customers are of Hispanic or Latino heritage, but only 22 percent of current board members are of this background. Nearly 50 percent of customers are over sixty years of age, and there are no representatives of that age group. The addition of two new programs serving younger families suggests the value of considering adding board representatives under thirty years of age.

Diversity definitions

There are many definitions of *diversity*. The working definition for this plan is the following: "differences that significantly affect the way we experience ourselves and are treated by others, especially people of a different ethnicity, ability, and age from the current majority." This definition may be revised during cultural competence training and planning sessions.

The terms *Mexican American*, *Latino*, *Chicano*, and *Hispanic* are highly political and should be further studied and addressed by the diversity team. For the purposes of this plan, the term *Latino* will be used to encompass all persons of Spanish-speaking heritage of both genders, as is current common practice in California. This term may not have wide acceptance in other areas where *Hispanic* is still in common use. In each part of the country and the world, key leaders can advise on current and appropriate terminology.

Benefits of diversity to strong governance

This section is based on National Center for Nonprofit Boards advanced consulting curriculum 2001.

National studies show that board diversity creates valuable attributes:

- *Creative problem solving.* Diverse group members offer alternatives to standard approaches.
- *A higher level of critical analysis.* Diverse perspectives and varied approaches are considered.
- *More creative thinking.* There is a reduced emphasis on conformity to norms of the past.
- *Diverse, complementary skills.* These skills promote innovation.

Board diversity plan goals

To ensure success, a board diversity plan must set specific goals, such as the following:

- Diversity will be embraced proactively as a core institutional value and embedded in every aspect of board work and planning.
- Training and systems that support excellence in diversity planning and implementation will be sustained by both staffing and funding.
- The board diversity commitment will be marketed effectively internally and externally.
- Diversity plan and goals will be evaluated objectively as well as by self-assessment.

Objectives and outcomes

Specific objectives with measurable outcomes might include some of the following:

- A standing committee of the board will take responsibility for ensuring adequate board composition as to diversity and all other qualifications. This committee will be called the *governance committee*.
- Internal training will be provided to the current board and management staff, creating an environment that welcomes diversity proactively, prior to recruitment of new board candidates.
- The board will adopt and publicize a diversity commitment statement.
- Diversity goals will be achieved in priority order as recommended by the diversity team, starting with ethnic and age diversity recruitment.
- A board mentorship plan will be put in place. All new board members will be matched with mentors for their first year on the board.
- Diversity and cultural competence board training will be provided annually.

Diversity plan implementation

An effective plan must contain implementation strategies. For each goal, there should be objectives, and for each objective, a list of tasks with clearly assigned responsibilities, time line, and evaluation method. A supporting budget for each element that requires additional personnel and materials is essential to achieving results.

Diversity team and governance committee description

A diversity team will oversee the implementation of the diversity plan by the governance committee. This team will include representatives of the groups being recruited, as well as no more than two majority culture representatives who are trained in, experienced with, and committed to diversity work. Team members may be recruited from outside the board if necessary to achieve this balance.

In addition to being responsible for overseeing the implementation of the diversity plan, the governance committee will be responsible for overseeing the implementation of the board development plan and ongoing board development activities, including board orientation, training, and self-assessment.

Evaluation and training

The full board will evaluate the success of the composition and functions of the governance committee in monitoring the board development plan and in meeting the board diversity plan goals. Training to be provided will include welcoming diversity and creating a culturally competent environment, and prospecting and recruiting board members with focus on diversity.

References

Association of Fundraising Professionals. "Chapter Diversity Best Practices." [http://www.afpnet.org/tier3_cd.cfm?content_item_id=3805&folder_id= 1645]. January 1, 2001.

Changing Our World. *Observations in Philanthropy*, Nov. 21, 2000 [www.changingourworld.com].

Changing Our World. *Observations in Philanthropy*. [E-mail newsletter from http://www.changingourworld.com]. Nov. 24, 2001.

Chait, R. P., Holland, T. P., Taylor, B. E. *Improving the Performance of Governing Boards*. Phoenix: Oryx Press, 1999.

Fischer, M. Executive Leadership Institute presentation, Center on Philanthropy, Indianapolis, May 1995.

Gardner, J. "National Renewal." Presentation to the National Civic League, Philadelphia, Nov. 12, 1994.

Gitin, M., and Stephens, C. R. "The Religious Challenge in Philanthropy." *Advancing Philanthropy*, Mar. 1999, pp. 18–23.

Hunt, A. R. "The Phony Protest . . . and Leaders." *Wall Street Journal*, Jan. 10, 2002, p. A13.

Maria Gitin & Associates. *Diversity in Fundraising Curriculum*. Capitola, Calif.: Maria Gitin & Associates, 1997.

Miller, J., Fletcher, K., and Abzug, R. *Perspectives on Nonprofit Board Diversity*. Washington, D.C.: National Center for Nonprofit Boards, 1999.

National Asian Pacific American League. [http://www.napalc.org/programs/antiviolence/pr/audit_release_3-11-02.htm].

National Center for Nonprofit Boards. *The Nonprofit Governance Index*. Washington, D.C.: National Center for Nonprofit Boards, 1999.

National Center for Nonprofit Boards. California Board Summit Report, 2000.

Payton, R. *Voluntary Action for the Public Good*. Washington, D.C.: American Council on Education, 1988.

Pementel, O. R. *Salinas Californian*, Jan. 9, 2002.

Princeton Survey Research Associates. "Taking America's Pulse II." Paper presented at the National Conference on Community and Justice, New York, 2000.

Sievers, B. "Can Philanthropy Solve the Problems of Civil Society?" *Philanthropy Journal*, Spring 1995.

Stern, G. *The Courage to Lead: Self-Assessment Tool, Presenter Guide*. New York: Drucker Foundation, 2001.

West, C. *Race Matters*. Boston: Beacon Press, 1993, p. 4.

Wolff, E. N. "Recent Trends in Wealth Ownership." Paper presented at the Benefits and Mechanisms for Spreading Asset Ownership in the United States conference, New York University, New York, Dec. 10–12, 1998.

YWCA of the U.S.A. "Our Mission." [http://www.ywca.org/html/B4a.asp]. 2002.

MARIA GITIN *is principal of Maria Gitin & Associates, an independent consulting group specializing in strategic planning, fundraising, and board development, with a focus on diversity and building capacity for fund development. Gitin is a senior trainer for Board Source/National Center for Nonprofit Boards Governance Project and a presenter for the Drucker Foundation.*

Nonprofit organizations should be governed and managed by representative numbers of their constituents but not limited to certain groups of people. Even organizations founded to empower or serve specific groups should have governing boards and managers that can look at issues from a range of different points of view.

5

Five reasons for nonprofit organizations to be inclusive

Samuel N. Gough, Jr.

AS THE DEMOGRAPHICS of the United States change, all sectors of society are displaying an increasing interest in the range of race, religion, nationality, and ethnicity now represented throughout the country. And, as the female to male ratio is nearly equal, there is a need to ensure a greater embodiment of the interests and needs of both genders in the nonprofit sector.

Acceptance of these facts influences the way that equality and equity should be viewed, the way that nonprofit organizations are governed and operated, and the way that they carry out their missions. This is true not just for legal, moral, and ethical reasons; of equal importance is the role of equality and equity in the accomplishment of missions and visions.

Recognition of these differences is often measured in terms of "diversity." The Association of Fundraising Professionals (formerly the National Society of Fund Raising Executives) defines *diversity*

NEW DIRECTIONS FOR PHILANTHROPIC FUNDRAISING, NO. 34, WINTER 2001 © WILEY PERIODICALS, INC.

in *The NSFRE Fund-Raising Dictionary* as "1. [T]he quality of being different. 2. The quality or state of encompassing people of a different race, gender, religion, physical disability, age, sexual orientation, and income" (Levy, 1996).

A logical question that this definition poses is, "Different from whom or what and different in what ways?" However, the word *different* might conjure up a negative image in the minds of some people. Therefore a more broadly acceptable definition might be "the inclusion of people of any gender, ethnicity, or age, covering a range of races, nationalities, religions, physical and mental abilities, sexual orientations, and income levels."

While nonprofit organizations adjust their missions to meet the demands of societal changes, they should be sure that they are inclusive of the range of people who use their services or whose lives they affect. *Webster's New World College Dictionary* (1997) refers the reader to the definition of *include*, which is "to have as part of a whole, contain, comprise." Therefore it is incumbent on nonprofit organizations to be inclusive. Inclusiveness means consideration of and accommodation for the distinctions that exist among people.

A useful definition of *nonprofit organization* also appears in *The NSFRE Fund-Raising Dictionary:* "[an organization] that pertains to or provides services of benefit to the public without financial incentive. A not-for-profit [nonprofit] organization is qualified by the Internal Revenue Service as a tax-exempt organization." The same source defines *public* as "any group of people that an organization seeks to influence for purposes such as using the organization's services, supporting the organization, endorsing its interests, or participating in the organization as employees or volunteers" (Levy, 1996). These two definitions provide reasons why nonprofit organizations should ensure that they are inclusive in all matters that pertain to the discharge of their missions.

Look beyond the usual borders

People often feel most comfortable associating with other people with whom they share similarities. This fact has the possibility both to enhance and to inhibit an organization's ability to attain its mission.

If the mission of an organization is to empower or to advance a particular segment of society, is the attainment of that mission more likely or less likely to be reached by having a governing board and staff members who are representative of that group of people? Should not those people, who are to be empowered, be involved in the efforts being expended to empower them? Should other people not a part of that group have an influence on the policies and management of the organization?

The nonprofit sector is replete with organizations that serve the needs of specific religious, ethnic, and racial groups and specific nationalities. Are the governing boards and senior staff of these organizations composed only of people of the same religious, ethnic, or racial group or nationality? If not, why not? If so, in what ways?

When governing board and staff members have shared values among themselves based only on their mutual similarities, actions may be taken quickly with a minimum of background briefings or explanations. For expediency this practice works well. However, it also might result in tunnel vision or overlooking critical facts when governing boards and staff members are chosen, decisions are made, and plans are formulated, without taking into consideration the full impact of those actions. Most often organizations benefit from the varied views of people with a range of backgrounds and experiences.

Care should be taken to ensure that organizations reflect the range of people whom they seek to serve. These organizations should be governed and managed by representative numbers of their constituents, not limited only to certain groups of people who do not relate directly to the purpose for which the organization exists. Even organizations that were founded to empower or to serve people of a specific race, religion, ethnicity, national origin, or gender should have governing boards and managers that can look at issues from a range of different points of view based on their backgrounds and experiences.

In some cases, it might be wise to create an advisory committee composed of people with experience and expertise that are not present on the governing board. Members of this committee would be recruited for a specific purpose or purposes that would not include establishing vision or mission statements, setting policy, or having fiduciary and legal responsibilities.

Increasingly, foundations and other funding sources ask organizations seeking their support about the racial and gender composition of the people who serve on their governing boards and staffs. The unspoken message that these questions send is that you are most likely to get our support if you have significant involvement of people with varied knowledge and expertise.

Appreciate other traditions of philanthropy

The 2000 U.S. census data reveal that there were 281,421,906 people counted. Ten and one-half million people said that they speak little or no English. Over the previous decade there was a growing share of foreign-born residents in the United States. A significant number of these people speak little or no English. Immigrants and the children of immigrants accounted for the fastest growth in the population. Simply for matters of communication, it is important that nonprofit organizations include people who can communicate with these potential constituents.

Nationwide, according to the 2000 census, 18 percent of residents spoke a language other than English at home. More than one-third of the people in California over the age of five were reported to have little mastery of English—the highest proportion in the country. New Mexico ranks second at 36 percent, and Texas follows with 32 percent. In the District of Columbia, 18,000 people reported a lack of proficiency in English. When the Maryland and Virginia suburbs are included, that number is increased to 232,000 people.

A sizable number of the immigrants, both legal and illegal, are in the United States for short periods of time. Very often there is little or no incentive for them to learn English. Also, for many of them, there is a reluctance to do anything that might bring undue attention to themselves or their family members. This especially includes seeking government services.

Early in his administration, President George W. Bush advocated granting amnesty to certain groups of illegal immigrants. That initiative lost its political impetus following the events of September 11, 2001. Many of the attitudes about foreign-born residents in this country changed following that day. What did not change were the political, economic, and social conditions that prompted an interest in changing immigration laws.

One example that might be noted is a nonprofit organization on the East Coast that provides health care referrals to immigrant parents who are severely hampered because many of them lack proficiency with the English language. For various reasons, these parents do not seek information about or help with the health services available to their children. Therefore many sick children go untreated, and if their illnesses are communicable, they are spread throughout the community. It is not that these parents do not care about the health of their children. They simply lack information, and they may be afraid to ask how to get help with or information on preventive measures.

The limitations in communicating in English may not affect the ability or the inclination of immigrants to give. The traditions of giving often are strong throughout most immigrant cultures. The key is to know what those traditions are. In many cultures giving is focused on supporting family members and religion. It is estimated that immigrants who live full or part time in the United States send billions of dollars annually to family members back in their home countries. This practice of giving indicates that there is a strong propensity to give in immigrant communities.

Two examples of the origins of philanthropy in other cultures from *Cultivating Diversity in Fundraising* by Janice Gow Pettey (2002) illustrate this point. She points out that the charitable traditions in Filipino communities are centered on support from the family and the extended family and based on a sense of responsibility. Spanish rule and the Catholic Church also have been influences in Filipino giving and sharing. Godparents *(compadres)*—the godfather *(ninong)* and the godmother *(ninang)*—are examples of the extended family. The system of this relationship is called *compadrazgo. Compadrazgo* often are successful members of the community who are expected to provide financial support for their godchildren. Filipinos in the United States sent an estimated $8 billion in 1989 to family members in the Philippines. Family members used this money not only for living expenses but also to help towns and neighborhoods, schools, hospitals, and churches.

The concept of giving and sharing for Japanese Americans can be traced to the influence of the Buddhist and Confucian religions in Japan (Pettey, 2002). The internment of Japanese Americans during World War II was a defining factor for Japanese Americans to give and to share among themselves. Prior to their internment, most first-generation Japanese Americans ("issei") were wage-earning adults who were raising second-generation ("nisei") children, the first to be born in the United States. However, when Japanese Americans were forced into detention camps, family life and customs were changed. Families spent less time together. The roles of the issei changed, as did the respect that they had among the nisei.

Group activities and challenges arising from a lack of family privacy in the camps created gaps between the generations. The older generation was not seen as powerful or exalted by their children, as they previously had been. Much of the older generation's dignity and sense of self-worth were stripped away by the actions of the United States government. As a result, the nisei were more interested in getting on with their American lives than they were in the preservation of the traditional family. Thus there was some erosion of traditional values, giving, and sharing among the nisei.

In our multicultural, multiracial society, nonprofit organizations should be aware of the fact that non-English-speaking people are potential volunteers and donors, as well as users of their services. For nonprofit organizations to fully tap the potential that exists in immigrant communities, lines of communication must be opened. These organizations must build on the established traditions of giving in the targeted community. They must have programs or services that are of interest to the individuals in that community, and they must involve those individuals in significant ways.

People support organizations with which they feel a connection. It is incumbent on the volunteers and staff members of the organizations seeking support to understand the traditions of giving and sharing of the people whose support they seek.

Recognize the power of women

Women should be viewed as an important asset at all levels of involvement in the programs, governance, and administration of nonprofit organizations. Studies have revealed enough differences between the philanthropic attitudes of women and men to prove that both genders should be included at all levels of nonprofit governance and management.

According to the U.S. Census Bureau data released March 15, 2001, there were 281,421,906 people in the United States. Over one-half—143,368,343—were women. And women outlive men by an average of seven years. Census data provide additional information that should be of interest to nonprofit organizations:

- Eighty-four percent of women age twenty-five and over have high school diplomas. That percentage is equal to the percentage for men.
- Twenty-four percent of women age twenty-five and over have a bachelor's degree or higher, compared with 28 percent for men.
- In 1999 the median earnings of women working full time, year-round was $26,324.
- Sixty-one percent of women age sixteen and over were in the civil labor force in March 2000, compared with 74 percent for men.
- Seventy-two percent of women age sixteen and over work in one of four occupations—administrative support (24 percent), professional specialty (18 percent), service worker other than private households (16 percent), and executive, administrative, and managerial (14 percent).

U.S. Census Bureau data (2000) reveal that women generated $2.1 trillion in earnings. In 1997, women held half of foundation CEO positions, 68 percent of program officer posts, and 93 percent of support staff positions, according to a 1998 Council on

Foundations survey of 667 foundations and corporate group programs. According to new data, the nonprofit sector accounts for 8 percent of the nation's Gross Domestic Product and employs nearly 10 percent of the work force—more than federal and state governments combined (http://www.pbs.org/ttc/society/philanthropy.html).

The Center for Women's Business Research (2000) issued a research summary titled *Survey Finds Business Owners Are Philanthropic Leaders: Women Entrepreneurs More Likely Than Men to Fill Leadership Roles as Volunteers for Charities*. In that report, Nina McLemore, chair of the National Foundation for Women Business Owners (NFWBO), makes the following observations from a survey conducted by INDEPENDENT SECTOR in 1999: "Nine out of ten business owners (92% of women and 88% of men) contribute money to charities, compared to 70 percent of all U.S. households. She goes on to note, "Nearly one-third of the business owners surveyed by NFWBO (31% of women, 30% of men) make significant personal charitable contributions of $5,000 or more per year, including 15% and 13%, respectively, who contribute $10,000 or more."

The research summary (Center for Women's Business Research, 2000) goes on to state: "Women and business owners who contribute and volunteer have increased their philanthropy in recent years. Fully half (52%) of women business owners state that their level of financial support has increased over the past five years, and 51% say that the hours devoted to charitable activities have likewise increased. Among men, 485 say their financial support has increased, and 39% say that the time devoted to charitable activities has increased."

According to the Gallup Organization (1986), "In families with incomes of $25,000 or more, black women are more likely to give to charity than white women are, and give in excess of $1,000. In addition, minorities are more likely to give when asked for a donation, but are asked less often than whites."

These statistics only scratch the surface of the contributions that women can and do make to the nonprofit community. Nonprofit organizations should note the giving patterns of women and gear their appeals to those patterns.

Consider the importance of religion

Although it may not be recommended that board or staff members be selected on the basis religious beliefs, often there are decided benefits to be derived when the decision makers represent a broad range of religious doctrines.

Every religion has some facet of its beliefs that distinguishes it from the others, and the people who profess these beliefs bring a wide range of ideas, experiences, and knowledge to the activities in which they are involved. However, religious convictions have the greatest potential for the creation of disagreements. Therefore when people are brought together to work for a common cause in which they have a mutual responsibility, care must be taken to ensure that there is tolerance, understanding, and respect for thoughts and actions that are based on religious tenets. When this occurs, the organizations that they serve are strengthened.

For the past fifty years, the U.S. census has not asked questions about religion. Statistics about religion and religious affiliation, when collected, are compiled by nongovernmental organizations. According to Robinson (2001), "There are more different religious groups in the United States than anywhere else on Earth. The remarkable diversity of religion in the United States makes it difficult to arrive at a good way to group them into manageable categories."

US Society and Values magazine published an overview of religion in the United States (Robinson, 1997), using data from the Pluralism Project at Harvard University. It reported that 63 percent of Americans (163 million) state that they are actively affiliated with a faith group:

- Roman Catholicism is the largest single religion, at 23 percent.
- Anglicans, Eastern Orthodox, and Protestant churches total 36 percent, which includes 220 denominations.
- There are 3.8 million religiously active Jews (1.5 percent); an additional 2 million regard themselves as cultural or ethnic Jews.
- Estimates of Muslims vary greatly. Some surveys show that there are about 3.5 to 3.8 million Muslims (1.4 to 1.5 percent)

in the United States. Most Muslims sources estimate about 6 or 7 million.

• Islam is numerically the fastest growing organized religion in the United States.

With regard to spiritual beliefs, the most rapidly growing group in the United States is not an organized religion; it consists of atheists and agnostics.

The Graduate Center of the City University of New York conducted an American religious identification survey (Kosmin, Mayer, and Keysar, 2001); it was a massive poll, questioning 50,281 American adults about their religious affiliations. They obtained some results that are noticeably different from the Pluralism Project's data. The differences are mainly because they asked their poll subjects what religion they considered themselves to be rather than what they were actually affiliated with. Results included the following:

• 52 percent of Americans identified themselves as Protestant
• 24 percent were Catholic
• 14.1 percent did not follow any organized religion
• 1.3 percent were Jewish
• 0.5 percent were Muslim or followers of Islam

In contrast, the Harris Interactive Election 2000 survey (Henderson, 2000) polled 13,224 registered voters selected at random from the Harris Interactive Internet Panel of more than 5.6 million respondents. The sample size was only 10 percent of the 1990 National Survey of Religious Identification, but it is considered statistically large enough to be accurate. (However, the sample population consisted of Internet users, and not all Americans have access to the Internet.) The purpose of this survey was to determine how religious affiliation would affect the 2000 presidential election. Although it was not conducted to determine religious affiliation, conclusions about religious affiliations might be drawn. Results of the survey are presented in Table 5.1.

Table 5.1. Results of the Harris Interactive Election 2000 survey

Affiliation	Number of Respondents	Percentage of Registered U.S. Voters
Christian	9,478	71.0
All Protestants	6,544	49.5
Baptist	1,700	12.9
Southern Baptist	933	7.1
Methodist	1,081	8.2
Lutheran	515	3.9
Presbyterian	336	2.5
Episcopalian	221	1.7
Other denominations	1,674	12.7
Catholic	2,629	19.9
Latter-Day Saints	186	1.4
Jewish	305	2.3
Agnostic or atheist	944	7.1
Other	N/A	10.0
Nonreligious, no answer	N/A	10.0
Total	13,224	100.0

Source: Henderson (2000).

In addition, the results of a national survey reported by the Henry J. Kaiser Family Foundation and Harvard University ("Outlook," 2001) may be of interest:

There is one characteristic that an overwhelming majority of Americans said would bother them: if a family member married an atheist.

Overall, seven in 10 of the 1,709 randomly selected adults surveyed said they would be troubled if a member of their immediate family married someone who did not believe in God. Nearly four in 10—39 percent—said they probably would come to accept it, but 30 percent said they never would. About three in 10 respondents—31 percent—said it "would be fine with them" if a family member married an atheist, the poll found.

Therefore religious convictions, or the lack of religious convictions, may be a strong determinant in the decisions that are made and the actions that are taken on behalf of a nonprofit organization that has no mission or vision directly related to a belief or lack of belief in a higher being. In other words, the core values that individuals form with regard to beliefs affect the thoughts and actions individuals have and take in most aspects of their lives. Decisions and behavior result from those core values.

An example of such an organization that makes decisions based on core values is the Washington Project, located in Washington, D.C. It is a 501(c)(3) faith-based organization providing entrepreneurship training and skills acquisition to individuals in the greater Washington metropolitan area. Economic development in urban markets is a severely needed process to promote the well being of the community. This organization's economic development programs provide a meaningful and holistic solution for revitalizing the under-served community.

The organization's mission "is to promote entrepreneurship for people who lack access to resources to attain their dreams for self-sufficiency through a coalition of Washington, DC area churches and community organizations." Its vision "is to break the cycle of poverty for individuals and families through the application of faith-based values that promote economic empowerment."

The Washington Project was founded "in 1998, when a coalition of churches and community organizations came together, with an interest in providing a means to become self-employed for people who lack access to resources. Such resources include capital, markets, and education. Together, these groups launched [the organization], which offers a variety of business training and support services. [The organization] works primarily within churches that are connected with the target audience [it] seeks to reach. The churches have demonstrated a committed, trusted, and supportive environment in which under-served individuals are already participating to access resources they need."

There has been a concerted effort to be inclusive in the selection of board members who represent various Protestant religious philosophies on the basis of the principles on which the organization was founded. This approach also has expanded the range of potential funding opportunities. In theory, the mission and the vision are broad enough to allow it to move beyond its current focus on seeking board members and funding from Protestants to anyone who shares the same mission and vision that the organization espouses. Whether that theory expands beyond non-Christian religions is yet to be seen. However, the same standard might be applied by other organizations as they build their volunteer and funding bases.

Another example to study is the mission statement of the National Conference for Community and Justice (NCCJ): "The National Conference for Community and Justice, founded in 1927 as The National Conference of Christians and Jews, is a human relations organization dedicated to fighting bias, bigotry and racism in America. NCCJ promotes understanding and respect among all races, religions and cultures through advocacy, conflict resolution and education" (National Conference for Community and Justice, 2002).

Its public policy vision statement affirms the direction that it takes regarding promoting understanding and respect throughout all strata of society (NCCJ, 2002):

The vision of The National Conference for Community and Justice's public policy program is to be a national resource to government, the media, and public, private and independent sector institutions on the issues central to our mission.

As a human relations organization dedicated to fighting bias, bigotry and racism through advocacy, conflict resolution and education, NCCJ is committed to providing credible research, articulating principles and values derived from the mission, convening people for civil discourse on public policy issues and disseminating accurate educational materials. Recent public policy initiatives include the distribution of information on how communities can respond to the presence of hate groups, the formulation of guidelines for religion in the public schools, and statements on immigration, affirmative action, welfare reform and the religious right.

The NCCJ's national board of directors and national advisory board are reflective of this nation's pluralistic society. The NCCJ conscientiously looks at religion as it involves people in the attainment of its mission.

Involve people based on what they can bring to the organization

There are so many areas of difference among people and so much assimilation that ethnicity, national origin, and race often are difficult to determine. The 2000 U.S. census allowed people to select from among sixty-three combinations of categories. *National origin* refers to the country of a person's birth. *Ethnicity* makes reference to the common cultural heritage of a population subgroup and national origin, such as distinguished by customs, language, or common history.

When looking at the position on race put forth by Norman C. Sullivan of Marquette University in *Cultivating Diversity in Fundraising* (Pettey, 2002), a question is raised about what constitutes the differences among people. Sullivan points out the difficulties of classifying people according to race. A summary of a few points that he makes follows:

• People throughout the world have different physical attributes. Human beings may look different from one another in a number of ways, such as skin color, body form, nose shape, size of the lips, and hair texture. Human beings are also variable in more subtle ways, as in the variation that occurs in all proteins of the body and in DNA sequences. However, there is no consistent group of traits that can be used to say that one group of people is distinct from another group of people.

• A popularly accepted premise is that there are five or six races that correspond to the major geographical regions of the world. However, many anthropologists do not believe that there is any biological reality to the concept of race.

• The more features that are added, the greater the number of races in a classification system. If one scheme is based on skin color, one set of races will be identified. If hair texture is added to skin color, a different set of races will be identified. Add a third trait, and a new set of races emerges.

- If a racial classification system is based on skin color alone, then there might be a single race of people with dark skin in Africa and some parts of southern Asia. However, the people of southern India have facial features and hair that more closely resemble those of European populations than those of Africans.

Even the classification of race used in the 2000 U.S. census is questionable. For example, "White refers to people having origins in any of the original peoples of Europe, the Middle East, or North Africa. It includes people who indicated their race or races as 'White' or who wrote in entries such as Irish, German, Polish, Italian, Lebanese, Near Easterner, or Arab" (U.S. Census, 2000). Thus, if skin color is a prime determinant, some people with these backgrounds become suspect under this definition.

These observations, however, should not be a reason for nonprofit organizations to disregard the importance of striving for racial, ethnic, and national origin balance. As they seek volunteers and donors, decisions should be based on the range of other qualifications that they have, such as interest in the organization's mission and vision, the ability to contribute to the attainment of that mission, and the professional expertise and skills that they have. Nonprofit organizations benefit when there is heterogeneity among volunteers, including governing board members, and on their staffs.

A checklist for inclusiveness

Nonprofit organizations that are committed to inclusion should consider the following recommendations:

- Be sure that all policies, practices, programs, services, and activities promote equity and equality regarding gender, ethnicity, and age, and include a range of races, nationalities, religions, physical and mental abilities, sexual orientations, and income levels.

- Include these same categories of people in the decision-making process and the implementation of the organization's policies.
- Be knowledgeable of the cultural traditions on which potential donors rely when they consider appeals for their time, expertise, and contributions.
- Broaden volunteer, staff, and donor prospect pools to ensure inclusiveness.
- Offer volunteer, gift, and grant opportunities that appeal to people based on their philanthropic traditions, interests, needs, and capabilities.
- Report regularly to all external constituents (donors and nondonors) on the commitment to the mission, the people involved, the fiscal condition of the organization, the use of funds raised, and plans for the future.

Summary

Nonprofit organizations can increase their levels of success by being inclusive in the following ways:

- Involving people with divergent points of view
- Recognizing that proficiency in the English language should not be a criterion for involvement
- Seeking the help of people of both genders
- Having a religious balance
- Striving for a racial, ethnic, and national origin balance

References

Center for Women's Business Research. *Survey Finds Business Owners Are Philanthropic Leaders: Women Entrepreneurs More Likely Than Men to Fill Leadership Roles as Volunteers for Charities.* Washington, D.C.: Center for Women's Business Research, 2000.

Gallup Organization. *The Contemporary Charitable Giving and Volunteerism of Black Women.* Princeton, N.J.: Gallup Organization, 1986.

Henderson, C. "Poll Finds Religion Rules in Campaign 2000." [http://christianity.about.com/library/weekly/aa052100.htm]. May 2000.

Kosmin, B. A., Mayer, E., and Keysar, A. "American Religious Identification Survey 2001." [http://www.gc.cuny.edu/studies/aris.pdf]. Dec. 2001.

Levy, B. (ed.). *The NSFRE Fund-Raising Dictionary.* New York: Wiley, 1996.

National Conference for Community and Justice. Mission statement. [http://www.nccj.org/nccj3.nsf/?Open]. 2002.

National Conference for Community and Justice. Policy vision statement. [http://www.nccj.org/missionstatement]. 2002.

"Outlook." *Washington Post,* July 22, 2001, p. B1.

Pettey, J. G. *Cultivating Diversity in Fundraising.* New York: Wiley, 2002.

Robinson, B. A. "Memberships of Various U.S. Religious Groups." [http://www.religioustolerance.org/us_rel.htm]. 2001.

Robinson, B. A. "U.S. Society and Values," [http://usinfo.state.gov/journals/itsv/0397/ijse/ijse0397.htm] 1997, p.1.

U.S. Census Bureau. "Introduction to Census 2000 Data—United States." [http://www.census.gov/population]/language/table1.txt]. 2000.

Webster's New World College Dictionary. (3rd ed.) New York: Macmillan, 1997.

SAMUEL N. GOUGH, JR., *is a principal with the AFRAM Group, a full-service development firm. After retiring from his alma mater, Howard University, he served as special assistant to the president for development at the National Council of Negro Women, in addition to working for the Children's Defense Fund, National Society of Fund Raising Executives, and the Thelonius Monk Institute of Jazz.*

INDEX

Back Issue/Subscription Order Form

Copy or detach and send to:
Jossey-Bass, 989 Market Street, San Francisco, CA 94103-1741

Call or fax toll free!
Phone 888-378-2537 6ᴀᴍ-5ᴘᴍ PST; Fax 888-481-2665

Back issues: Please send me the following issues at $28 each
(Important: please include series initials and issue number, such as PF10)

1. PF _____

_____

_____

$ _____ Total for single issues

$ _____ SHIPPING CHARGES: SURFACE   Domestic   Canadian

		SURFACE	Domestic	Canadian
	First Item		$5.00	$6.00
	Each Add'l Item		$3.00	$1.50

For next-day and second-day delivery rates, call the number listed above.

Subscriptions   Please ❑ start   ❑ renew my subscription to *New Directions for Philanthropic Fundraising* at the following rate:

US: ❑ Individual $75   ❑ Institutional $147
Canada: ❑ Individual $75   ❑ Institutional $187
All others: ❑ Individual $99   ❑ Institutional $221

NOTE: Issues are published quarterly. Subscriptions are for the calendar year only. Subscriptions begin with the Spring issue. Add appropriate sales tax for your state for single issue orders. No sales tax for U.S. subscriptions.

$ _____ Total single issues and subscriptions (Canadian residents, add GST for subscriptions and single issues)

❑ Payment enclosed (U.S. check or money order only)

❑ VISA, MC, AmEx, Discover Card # _____ Exp. date_____

Signature _____ Day phone _____

❑ Bill me (U.S. institutional orders only. Purchase order required)

Purchase order # _____

Federal Tax ID 135593032   GST 89102-8052

Name _____

Address _____

_____

Phone _____ E-mail _____

For more information about Jossey-Bass, visit our Web site at:
www.josseybass.com   **PRIORITY CODE = ND1**

Previous Issues Available